DAYBOOK

OF CRITICAL READING AND WRITING

daybook, *n.* a book in which the events of the day are recorded; *specif.* a journal or diary

THE AUTHORS
* Fran Claggett
* Louann Reid
* Ruth Vinz

Great Source Education Group
A division of Houghton Mifflin Company
Wilmington, Massachusetts

THE AUTHORS

❊ **Fran Claggett**, an educational consultant, writer, and teacher at Sonoma State University, taught high school and college English for more than thirty years. Her books include *Drawing Your Own Conclusions: Graphic Strategies for Reading, Writing, and Thinking* (1992) with Joan Brown, *A Measure of Success* (1996), and *Teaching Writing: Art, Craft, and Genre* (2005) with Joan Brown, Nancy Patterson, and Louann Reid.

❊ **Louann Reid** taught junior and senior high school English for nineteen years and currently teaches courses for future English teachers at Colorado State University. She has edited *English Journal* and is the author or editor of several books and articles, including *Learning the Landscape and Recasting the Text* (1996) with Fran Claggett and Ruth Vinz. She is a frequent consultant and workshop presenter nationally and internationally.

❊ **Ruth Vinz**, currently a professor of English education and Morse Chair in Teacher Education at Teachers College, Columbia University, taught in secondary schools for twenty-three years. She is author of numerous books and articles that focus on teaching and learning in the English classroom. Dr. Vinz is a frequent presenter at conferences as well as a consultant and co-teacher in schools throughout the country.

REVIEWERS

Lorraine Becker
Cherry Creek Schools
Centennial, CO

Diann Cohen
Springfield Public Schools
Springfield, MA

Fran Ennis
Lake Stevens School District
Lake Stevens, WA

Patricia A. Fair
Cherry Creek Schools
Greenwood Village, CO

Beth Gaby
Chicago Public Schools
Chicago, IL

Connie McGee
Pembroke Pines, FL

Geraldine Ortego
Lafeyette Parish
Lafayette, LA

Elizabeth Rehberger
Huntington Beach, CA

EDITORIAL: Barbara Levadi and Sue Paro
DESIGN AND PRODUCTION: AARTPACK, Inc.

Printed in the United States of America

International Standard Book Number 13: 978-0-669-53483-2

4 5 6 7 8 9 10 0956 13 12 11 10 09

Contents

 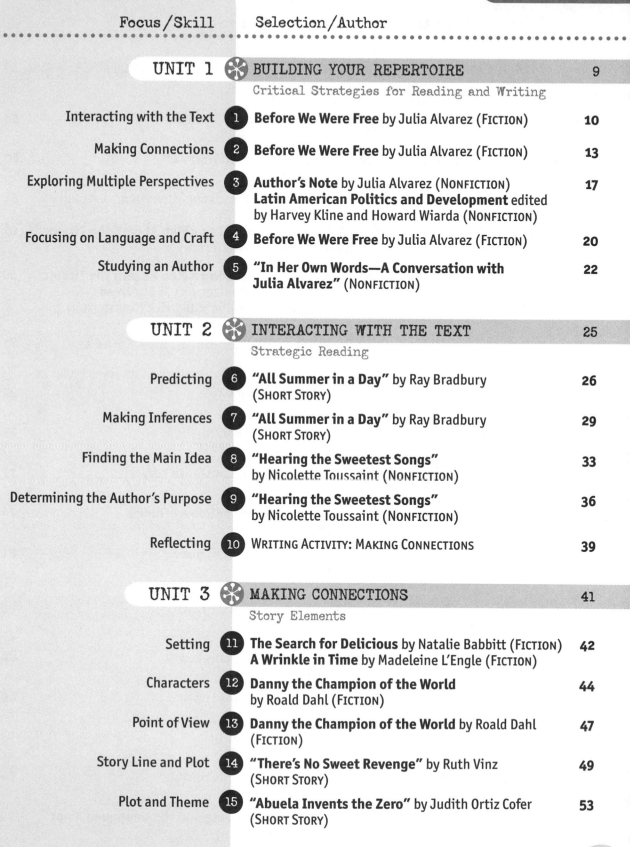

Focus/Skill		Selection/Author	

Focus/Skill		Selection/Author	

Building Your Repertoire

Think about something you do well—playing baseball, skateboarding, singing, drawing, or playing an instrument. What did you do to become good at this activity? You probably learned all the skills necessary to excel. You practiced. You built a **repertoire,** or a collection, of essential skills and strategies to perform effectively. Good readers and writers build a **repertoire of skills and strategies,** too. The goal of this unit is to help you develop a repertoire of five useful approaches to reading and writing.

Throughout this *Daybook*, you will read, respond to, and write about many different kinds of texts. You will read and write for a variety of purposes. You'll circle, underline, and highlight what you read. You will make guesses, ask questions, predict, and talk about meaning with others. You'll draw pictures, make charts, and brainstorm. You will do some writing of your own. In short, you will build a repertoire of actions that are the tools to help you read actively and write effectively.

INTERACTING WITH THE TEXT

Reading is like having a conversation. Instead of talking to a person, you have a conversation with the words and ideas on the page. **Interacting with the text** is like carrying on a conversation with what you are reading. When you interact, you are actively involved in your reading. Reading with your pen is one way to record how your mind works while you are reading. There is space in the **Response Notes** for you to have a conversation. As you read, react to what is going on by circling, underlining, and writing notes.

The selection below is from a novel about a young girl, Anita de la Torre, and her family. They live in the Dominican Republic in 1960. In the **Response Notes,** you will see how one reader used her pen to interact with the text.

from **Before We Were Free** by Julia Alvarez

Response Notes

Why is there an American School in the Dominican Republic?

"May I have some volunteers?" Mrs. Brown is saying. We are preparing skits for Thanksgiving, two weeks away. Although the Pilgrims never came to the Dominican Republic, we are attending the American school, so we have to celebrate American holidays.

It's a hot, muggy afternoon. I feel lazy and bored. Outside the window, the palm trees are absolutely still. Not even a breeze. Some of the American students have been complaining that it doesn't feel like Thanksgiving when it's as hot as the Fourth of July.

Mrs. Brown is looking around the room. My cousin, Carla, sits in the seat in front of me, waving her arm.

This doesn't seem fair

Mrs. Brown calls on Carla, and then on me. Carla and I are to play the parts of two Indians welcoming the Pilgrims. Mrs. Brown always gives the not-so-good parts to those of us in class who are Dominicans.

She hands us each a headband with a feather sticking up like one rabbit ear. I feel ridiculous. "Okay, Indians, come forward and greet the Pilgrims." Mrs. Brown motions toward where Joey Farland and Charlie Price stand with their toy rifles and the Davy Crockett hats they've talked Mrs. Brown into letting them wear. Even I know the pioneers come after the Pilgrims.

What do Davy Crockett hats look like?

"Anita"—she points at me—"I want you to say, 'Welcome to the United States.'"

Before I can mutter my line, Oscar Mancini raises his hand. "Why the Indians call it the United Estates when there was no United Estates back then, Mrs. Brown?"

Good point!

The class groans. Oscar is always asking questions. "United Estates! United Estates!" somebody in the back row mimics. Lots of classmates snicker, even some Dominicans. I hate it when the American kids make fun of the way we speak English.

"That's a good question, Oscar," Mrs. Brown responds, casting a disapproving look around. She must have heard the whisper as well. "It's called poetic license. Something allowed in a story that isn't so in real life. Like a metaphor or a simile."

Just then, the classroom door opens. I catch a glimpse of our principal, and behind him, Carla's mother, Tía Laura, looking very nervous. But, then, Tía Laura always looks nervous. Papi likes to joke that if there were ever an Olympic event for worrying, the Dominican Republic would win with his sister on the team. But lately, Papi looks pretty worried himself. When I ask questions, he replies with "Children should be seen, not heard" instead of his usual "Curiosity is a sign of intelligence."

Mrs. Brown comes forward from the back of the room and stands talking to the principal for a few minutes before she follows him out into the hall, where Tía Laura is standing. The door closes.

Usually when our teacher leaves the room, Charlie Price, the class clown, acts up. He does stuff like changing the hands on the clock so that Mrs. Brown will be all confused and let us out for recess early. Yesterday, he wrote NO HOMEWORK TONIGHT in big block letters above the date on the board, THURSDAY, NOVEMBER 10, 1960. Even Mrs. Brown thought that was pretty funny.

But now the whole class waits quietly. The last time the principal came to our classroom, it was to tell Tomasito Morales that his mother was here for him. Something had happened to his father, but even Papi, who knew Señor Morales, would not say what. Tomasito hasn't come back to school since then.

Beside me, Carla is tucking her hair behind her ears, something she does when she's nervous. My brother, Mundín, has a nervous tic, too. He bites his nails whenever he does something wrong and has to sit on the punishment chair until Papi comes home.

The door opens again, and Mrs. Brown steps back in, smiling that phony smile grown-ups smile when they are keeping bad news from you. In a bright voice, Mrs. Brown asks Carla to please collect her things. "Would you help her, Anita?" she adds.

We walk back to our seats and begin packing up Carla's schoolbag. Mrs. Brown announces to the class that they'll continue with their skits later. Everyone is to take out his or her vocabulary book and start on the next chapter. The class pretends to settle down to its work, but of course, everyone is stealing glances at Carla and me.

Mrs. Brown comes over to see how we're doing. Carla packs her homework, but leaves the usual stay-at-school stuff in her desk.

"Are those yours?" Mrs. Brown points at the new notebooks, the neat lineup of pens and pencils, the eraser in the shape of the Dominican Republic.

Carla nods.

"Pack it all up, dear," Mrs. Brown says quietly.

We pack Carla's schoolbag with everything that belongs to her. The whole time I'm wondering why Mrs. Brown hasn't asked me to pack my stuff, too. After all, Carla and I are in the same family.

Oscar's hand is waving and dipping like a palm tree in a cyclone. But Mrs. Brown doesn't call on him. This time, I think we're all hoping he'll get a chance to ask his question, which is probably the same question that's in everyone's head: Where is Carla going? ✥

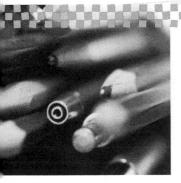

✳ Compare your **Response Notes** with a partner's. Add additional comments as a result of your discussion.

✳ Imagine that you have the opportunity to start a conversation in writing with one of the characters of *Before We Were Free*. Whom will you choose? What questions will you ask? Write a note to one of the characters.

When you interact with the text by jotting notes, asking questions, circling, highlighting, and stating reactions, you make it your own.

Make connections between what you are reading and what you know and have experienced in your life. What you read may remind you of movies you've seen or other books you've read. You can also relate what you are reading to news of world events or places in the world you've heard about. **Making connections** helps you understand what you are reading by comparing it to something you already know.

Read another excerpt from Alvarez's *Before We Were Free*. In the **Response Notes,** record any connections you make to the characters or events in the story.

from **Before We Were Free** by Julia Alvarez

We ride home in the Garcías' Plymouth with the silver fins that remind me of the shark I saw at the beach last summer. I'm stuffed in the back with Carla and her younger sisters, Sandi and Yo, who've been taken out of their classes, too. A silent and worried-looking Tía Laura sits in front next to Papi, who is driving.

"What's happening?" I keep asking. "Is something wrong?"

"*Cotorrita*," Papi warns playfully. That's my nickname in the family because sometimes I talk too much, like a little parrot, Mami says. But then at school, I'm the total opposite and Mrs. Brown complains that I need to speak up more.

Papi begins explaining that the Garcías have finally gotten permission to leave the country, and they'll be taking the airplane in a few hours to go to the United States of America. He's trying to sound excited, looking in the rearview mirror at us. "You'll get to see the snow!"

None of the García sisters says a word.

"And Papito and Mamita and all your cousins," Papi goes on. "Isn't that so, Laura?"

"*Sí, sí, sí,*" Tía Laura agrees. She sounds like someone letting air out of a tire.

My grandparents left for New York at the beginning of September. My other aunts and uncles were already there, having gone away with the younger cousins back in June. Who knows where Tío Toni is? Now, with the García cousins leaving, only my family will be left living at the compound.

I lean forward with my arms on the front seat. "So are we going to go, too, Papi?"

Papi shakes his head. "Somebody has to stay and mind the store." That's what he always says whenever he can't go on an outing because he has to work. Papito, my grandfather, started Construcciones de la Torre, a concrete-block business to build houses that won't blow over during hurricanes. When my grandfather retired a few years ago, Papi, being the oldest, was put in charge.

Response Notes

I was always told to speak up more in class, too.

Take a moment to write about the strongest connection you've
made so far.

_____

_____

_____

_____

_____

_____

_____

_____

_____

_____

The following scene occurs the day after Anita's cousins leave for
the United States. Papi and Anita's brother Mundín have already gone
to work. Anita, her mother, her sister, Lucinda, and Chucha, her old
nanny, are at home. As you read, continue recording connections in
your **Response Notes.**

**Response
Notes**

A half-dozen black Volkswagens are crawling up our driveway.

Before the cars come to a complete stop, the doors open, and a stream of
men pour out all over the property. In their dark glasses, they look like gangsters in the American movies that sometimes come to town.

I run to get Mami, but she's already headed for the door. Four men stand
in our entryway, all dressed in Khaki pants with small holsters at their belts
and tiny revolvers that don't look real.

The head guy—or at least he does all the talking—asks Mami for Carlos
García and his family. I know something is really wrong when Mami says,
"Why? Aren't they home?"

But then, instead of going away, this guy asks if his men can search our
house. Mami, who I'm sure will say, "Do you have a *permiso*?" steps aside like
the toilet is overflowing and these are the plumbers coming to the rescue!

I trail behind Mami, "Who are they?" I ask.

Mami swings around, a terrified look on her face, and hisses, "Not now!"

I race to find Chucha, who's in the entryway, shaking her head at the muddy boot prints. I ask her who these strange men are.

"SIM," she whispers. She makes a creepy gesture of cutting off her head with her index finger.

"But *who* are the SIM?" I ask again. I'm feeling more and more panicked at how nobody is giving me a straight answer.

"*Policia secreta*," she explains. "They go around investigating everyone and then disappearing them."

"*Secret* police?"

Chucha gives me her long, slow, guillotine nod that cuts off any further questions.

They go from room to room, looking in every nook and cranny. When they come through the hall door to the bedroom part of the house, Mami hesitates. "Just a routine search, *doña*," the head guy says. Mami smiles wanly, trying to show she has nothing to hide.

In my room, one guy lifts the baby-doll pajamas I left lying on the floor as if a secret weapon is hidden underneath. Another yanks the covers back from my bed. I hold on tight to Mami's ice-cold hand and she tightens her hold on mine.

The men go into Lucinda's room without knocking, opening up the jalousies, lifting the bedskirt and matching skirt on her vanity, plunging their bayonets underneath. My older sister sits up in bed, startled, her pink-foam rollers askew from sleeping on them. A horrible red rash has broken out on her neck.

When the men are done searching the room, Mami gives Lucinda and me her look that means business. "I want you both in here while I accompany our visitors," she says with strained politeness. ❖

In the table below, list the connections you made as you read. Share your lists with a partner. Add any other connections that come to mind as you discuss the lists.

Connections to you	Connections to other texts (books, movies, etc.)	Connections to world events, places, situations beyond your life

Make connections to your experiences, other texts, or a local, or world event to help you better understand what you are reading.

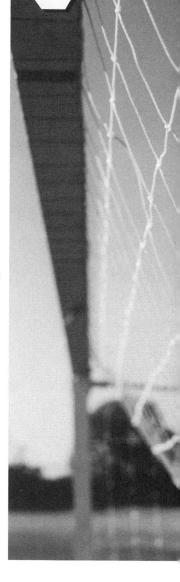

Almost anything can be seen from more than one perspective. A **perspective** is the point of view or angle from which you see a subject. If you are the goalie, you won't have the same perspective as a forward on the other team. Think about how you would describe winning the game if you blocked a final attempt to score. Then think how the player who tried to score might describe the same play. Both players participated in the same event, but they have different perspectives on what happened.

Try taking the approach of exploring multiple perspectives when you read. Notice who tells or writes about the events. Multiple perspectives give you a more complete version of an event.

On the pages that follow, you will explore three different perspectives to learn more about the events in Alvarez's story.

VANTAGE POINT 1

Character's Perspective: Who gets to tell the story?

Anita is the narrator of the story. We have her perspective on situations and events. To begin exploring multiple viewpoints, choose one of the other characters—Mami, Lucinda, Chucha, or one of the SIM— to tell the incident of the house search.

After you choose which character will narrate the scene, think about that person's point of view. For example, what might Mami think about during the search? What did Lucinda see as she was awakened by the SIM? What might any one of the SIMs think as they search the house?

Write in the present tense just as the author did to make your retelling seem as if it is happening right now.

_____

_____

_____

_____

_____

_____

_____

_____

_____

_____

VANTAGE POINT 2

Author's Perspective: What is the author's story?

Sometimes an author provides interesting information about the subject or tells the purpose of what she has written.

In your **Response Notes,** write what you learn from the author that helps you understand what is going on in the story. Share with a partner what you learned from the author.

Author's Note from *Before We Were Free* by Julia Alvarez

"I won't ever forget the day in 1960 when my parents announced that we were leaving our native country of the Dominican Republic for the United States of America. I kept asking my mother why we had to go. All she would say, in a quiet, tense voice, was "Because we're lucky."

Soon after our arrival in New York City, my parents explained why we had left our homeland in such a hurry. Many of the questions in my head began to be answered.

For over thirty years, our country had been under the bloody rule of General Trujillo. The secret police (SIM) kept tabs on everybody's doings. Public gatherings were forbidden. The least breath of resistance could bring arrest, torture, and death to you as well as your family. No one dared to disobey."

VANTAGE POINT 3

Historical Perspective: What's the history behind the story?

Before We Were Free is a historical novel, meaning it draws the fictional story from real events. Read the following excerpt from a historical account of the Dominican Republic that gives information about General Trujillo. Make notes that indicate what you learn that adds to your understanding of the story.

from Latin American Politics and Development

Harvey Kline and Howard Wiarda, editors

The thirty-one year rule of Rafael Trujillo has been described as Latin America's most complete dictatorship. The Dominican Republic was controlled by one man and his extended family from 1930 to 1961, and that control was often achieved through brutal repression. The Dominican Republic during the Trujillo years became a country in which opposition politics and dissent were crushed and democracy was transformed into a kind of cult of personality with *el presidente* as the center of the political system.

As the world became more aware of the repressive nature of Trujilloism, the system of control that he had built gradually came tumbling down. Opposition leaders and intellectuals became more forceful in their attacks on Trujillo, the United States tired of supporting an ally who had become an embarrassment, and most important, the middle class in the country came to realize that the leader's corruption and control were harming the economy and limiting their ability to advance. ❖

❋ Ask yourself: What information did this perspective or vantage point help me notice about the events or people in the story? In the space below, summarize something important you learned from each perspective you tried out.

VANTAGE POINT 1
Character's Perspective: Who gets to tell the story?

_____

_____

_____

_____

VANTAGE POINT 2
Author's Perspective: What is the author's story?

_____

_____

_____

_____

VANTAGE POINT 3
Historical Perspective: What's the history behind the story?

Examine multiple perspectives to learn more about and to evaluate what you are reading.

_____

_____

_____

If you tell your friend about something really exciting, you'll choose the right words to capture the important moments. You'll help your friend see and feel what you experienced.

Authors choose words and details to create pictures in the minds of their readers and to prompt responses from them. As you focus on how authors shape their language, you will focus on language and craft. **Description** is one of the basic techniques that an author uses to make scenes vivid for the reader.

Take a close look at another scene from the novel. This scene occurs shortly after the search took place. As you read, write reactions in your **Response Notes** and circle the descriptions that caused those reactions.

from **Before We Were Free** by Julia Alvarez

Response Notes

Must be a noisy motor!

Those black cars sit there for days and days—sometimes there's only one, sometimes as many as three. Every morning, when Papi leaves for the office, one of the cars starts up its (colicky motor) and follows him down the hill. In the evening, when he comes home, it comes back with him. I don't know when those SIM ever go to their own houses to eat their suppers and talk with their kids.

"Are they really policemen?" I keep asking Mami. It doesn't make any sense. If the SIM are policemen, secret or not, shouldn't we trust them instead of being afraid of them? But all Mami will say is "Shhh!" Meanwhile, we can't go to school because something might happen to us. "Like what?" I ask. Like what Chucha said about people disappearing? Is that what Mami worries will happen to us? "Didn't Papi say we should carry on with normal life?"

"Anita, *por favor*," Mami pleads, collapsing in a hall chair. She leans forward and whispers in my ear, "Please, please, you must stop asking questions."

"But why?" I whisper back. I can smell her shampoo, which smells like coconuts in her hair.

"Because I don't have any answers," she replies. ❖

✳ Draw one of the pictures that you have in your mind as you finish reading. Use the author's descriptions to guide you. Use pen, colored pencils, crayons, or markers.

✳ Share your sketch with a partner. Explain to each other how the author's descriptions helped you create pictures in your mind. Refer to your **Response Notes** to show specific descriptions that made the scene vivid.

✳ In the space below, draw a picture of an important person, pet, or event from your own life. Then describe what you have drawn. Choose words that will help create that picture in the mind of your reader.

Read to a partner what you have written. Ask your partner to tell you the picture that comes to his or her mind.

Examine how writers use descriptive language to help readers form pictures in their minds.

Authors often write about what they know. This doesn't mean that every book is an account of the author's life. However, many writers borrow bits and pieces from their lives. As you already know, Julia Alvarez draws heavily from her life experiences and from the time when she was a child living in the Dominican Republic. Taking the approach of studying an author offers a window into the writer's attitudes and beliefs. Knowing about the author's life might help you understand what motivates the ideas. You might see more fully what the author's attitudes are.

As you read the interview below, "In her own words—a conversation with Julia Alvarez," notice that there is a questioner **Q** and Julia Alvarez **A**. The questioner's comments are in **boldface** and the author's are not. Use your **Response Notes** to compare the information the author shares with the situation, events, and people in the novel.

from "In her own words—a conversation with Julia Alvarez"

Response Notes

Q **We learn in your author's note that this story was inspired by your own and your family's experience in the Dominican Republic. How much of a role did your own memories and the true stories you heard play in the writing of the book?**

Just like when Carla left class.

A My father was involved in the underground against the Trujillo dictatorship in the Dominican Republic. When members of his immediate "cell" were rounded up, we had to leave in a hurry for the United States. But my uncle, who was also involved in the underground, and his family remained. Some members of the group who assassinated the dictator went to my uncle's house to hide. When they were caught, my uncle was also taken away. My aunt and cousins lived under house arrest for nine months, not knowing if my uncle was dead or alive. He survived, but the members who had hidden in his house were killed by the dictator's son. These men were very close friends of my family. In fact, growing up, I called them *tíos*, uncles; their kids were my playmates. So you see, I had some connection to what actually happened. In writing the book, I conducted interviews with survivors, and I also read a lot of the history. I was particularly interested in the sons and daughters of those who had been tortured, imprisoned, or murdered—kids like my cousins and my childhood playmates. So it was a composite both of doing research and of remembering family stories.

Q In the book Anita's parents insist on staying in the country to fight for change. Have you continued to be committed to and involved in the future of the Dominican Republic? Do you view the writing of this book as a part of that commitment?

A Definitely. My husband and I now have an organic coffee farm [in the Dominican Republic] that is part of a cooperative of small farmers trying to save the land from erosion and pesticides. We set it up as a foundation so that the proceeds from the sale of our coffee go to fund a school on the farm. We did this when we realized that none of our neighbors could read or write: ninety-five percent illiteracy in that area! I feel so very lucky to have the opportunities we have in this country. But we can't stop there. We have a responsibility to those who are less lucky. I know I feel a special commitment to those who stayed behind in my native country, fighting for freedom and opportunities. The other way I'm still involved in my native land is by writing....

✳ Imagine that you have been asked to introduce Julia Alvarez—the writer and the person—to a group of students who will be reading *Before We Were Free*. What do you want to emphasize? What is most interesting to you? Write your introduction in the space below.

_____

_____

_____

_____

_____

_____

_____

_____

_____

_____

_____

_____

_____

_____

Response Notes

✳ Read another part of the conversation. Record your reactions in your **Response Notes.**

[Q] **Can learning about others and becoming more politically aware really make a difference? Where do we start?**

[A] . . . I often think of that biblical phrase: "The truth shall make you free," and also that wonderful quote, "Those who cannot remember the past are condemned to repeat it." Young people as well as older people need to know the stories of their families, their communities, their countries, each other, be-cause it's a way to be aware and experience the realities of others. In dictator-ships, there is always only one story: the official story no one can contradict. All other stories are silenced. It's the knowing of each other's stories and the feeling and compassion created by knowing these stories that connect us as individuals to each other and make a humane human family out of different populations and countries and ethnicities. ✤

✳ Alvarez challenges us to know the stories of our families and communities. She encourages us to share our stories with others. Use the space below to write a story of your family or community that you want to share with others.

> In order to understand why an author writes what he or she writes, learn what you can about the author's life and purposes for writing. This may also give you ideas for your own writing.

Interacting with the Text

What do you like to read? Fantasy? Science fiction? Mysteries? When you like what you're reading, you probably find it easy to understand.

But what happens when you have to read something new or difficult? That's when you need to become a **strategic reader.** Good readers use a repertoire of skills and strategies to help them understand what they read. Part of the repertoire is interacting with the text. When you interact with the text, you think about it and you write about it. In this unit, you will practice several strategies you can use to interact with the text.

Strategic readers interact with text by making predictions as they read to help them better understand events and characters. When you first read the title, you probably guess what the story will be about based on the words in the title and what you know about the title. That is a **prediction**. As you read further, you check to see if your prediction matches what the author wrote, or if you need to revise your prediction. Strategic readers predict and check several times while they read a story.

As you read the first part of Ray Bradbury's short story, "All Summer in a Day," use the **Response Notes** column to make notes about what you think might happen next and why. You will come back to your predictions after you finish the first part of the story.

"All Summer in a Day" by Ray Bradbury

Response Notes

"Ready?"

"Ready."

"Now?"

"Soon."

"Do the scientists really know? Will it happen today, will it?"

"Look, look; see for yourself!"

The children pressed to each other like so many roses, so many weeds, intermixed, peering out for a look at the hidden sun.

It rained.

It had been raining for seven years; thousands upon thousands of days compounded and filled from one end to the other with rain, with the drum and gush of water, with the sweet crystal fall of showers and the concussion of storms so heavy they were tidal waves come over the islands. A thousand forests had been crushed under the rain and grown up a thousand times to be crushed again. And this was the way life was forever on the planet Venus, and this was the schoolroom of the children of the rocket men and women who had come to a raining world to set up civilization and live out their lives.

"It's stopping, it's stopping!"

"Yes, yes!"

Margot stood apart from them, from these children who could never remember a time when there wasn't rain and rain and rain. They were all nine years old, and if there had been a day, seven years ago, when the sun came out for an hour and showed its face to the stunned world, they could not recall.

I think Margot knows something about the sun because she is different from the others.

Sometimes, at night, she heard them stir, in remembrance, and she knew they were dreaming and remembering gold or a yellow crayon or a coin large enough to buy the world with.

She knew that they thought they remembered a warmness, like a blushing in the face, in the body, in the arms and legs and trembling hands. But then they always awoke to the tatting drum, the endless shaking down of clear bead necklaces upon the roof, the walk, the gardens, the forests, and their dreams were gone.

All day yesterday they had read in class about the sun, about how like a lemon it was, and how hot. And they had written small stories or essays or poems about it:

I think the sun is a flower,

That blooms for just one hour.

That was Margot's poem, read in a quiet voice in the still classroom while the rain was falling outside.

"Aw, you didn't write that!" protested one of the boys.

"I did," said Margot. "I did."

"William!" said the teacher.

But that was yesterday. Now the rain was slackening, and the children were crushed in the great thick windows.

"Where's teacher?"

"She'll be back."

"She'd better hurry, we'll miss it!"

They turned on themselves, like a feverish wheel, all tumbling spokes.

Margot stood alone. She was a very frail girl who looked as if she had been lost in the rain for years and the rain had washed out the blue from her eyes and the red from her mouth and the yellow from her hair. She was an old photograph dusted from an album, whitened away, and if she spoke at all her voice would be a ghost. Now she stood, separate, staring at the rain and the loud wet world beyond the huge glass.

"What are you looking at?" said William.

Margot said nothing.

"Speak when you're spoken to." He gave her a shove. But she did not move; rather she let herself be moved only by him and nothing else.

They edged away from her, they would not look at her. She felt them go away. And this was because she would play no games with them in the echoing tunnels of the underground city. If they tagged her and ran, she stood blinking

after them and did not follow. When the class sang songs about happiness and life and games, her lips barely moved. Only when they sang about the sun and the summer did her lips move as she watched the drenched windows.

And then, of course, the biggest crime of all was that she had come here only five years ago from Earth, and she remembered the sun and the way the sun was and the sky was when she was four, in Ohio. And they, they had been on Venus all their lives, and they had been only two years old when last the sun came out and had long since forgotten the color and heat of it and the way it really was. But Margot remembered.

"It's like a penny," she said once, eyes closed.

"No, it's not!" the children cried.

"It's like a fire," she said, "in the stove."

"You're lying; you don't remember!" cried the children.

But she remembered and stood quietly apart from all of them and watched the patterning windows. And once, a month ago, she had refused to shower in the school shower rooms, had clutched her hands to her ears and over her head, screaming the water mustn't touch her head. So after that, dimly, dimly, she sensed it; she was different and they knew her difference and kept away. ✣

 Put check marks next to the events in the text where your pre-dictions were similar to the story. Using your notes, write one sentence predicting what will happen next and explain why.

_____

_____

_____

✳ Based on your prediction, continue the story as if you were the author.

_____

_____

_____

_____

_____

_____

_____

_____

Strategic readers constantly make predictions and check them when they read.

Have you ever read all the words and still felt that something was missing? Maybe you needed to interact with the text by reading "between the lines." Writers might not tell you everything you want to know. So strategic readers **make inferences** by putting together something they have read with something they already know. Remember when Bradbury wrote that William gave Margot a shove? He was counting on you to know about a time when a boy acted the same way so you could make an inference about the kind of person William is.

Read the next part of "All Summer in a Day" to see why that matters. Notice what William says and does. Jot down notes that tell what you learn about William and what you learn about the other children.

"All Summer in a Day" by Ray Bradbury (continued)

Response Notes

There was talk that her father and mother were taking her back to Earth next year; it seemed vital to her that they do so, though it would mean the loss of thousands of dollars to her family. And so, the children hated her for all these reasons, of big and little consequence. They hated her pale, snow face, her waiting silence, her thinness, and her possible future.

"Get away!" The boy gave her another push. "What're you waiting for?"

Then, for the first time, she turned and looked at him. And what she was waiting for was in her eyes.

"Well, don't wait around here!" cried the boy, savagely. "You won't see nothing!"

Her lips moved.

"Nothing!" he cried. "It was all a joke, wasn't it?" He turned to the other children. "Nothing's happening today. Is it?"

They all blinked at him and then, understanding, laughed and shook their heads.

"Oh, but," Margot whispered, her eyes helpless. "But this is the day, the scientists predict, they say, they know, the sun . . ."

"All a joke!" said the boy and seized her roughly. "Hey, everyone, let's put her in a closet before teacher comes!"

"No," said Margot, falling back.

They surged about her, caught her up and bore her, protesting, and then pleading, and then crying, back into a tunnel, a room, a closet, where they slammed and locked the door. They stood looking at the door and saw it tremble from her beating and throwing herself against it. They heard her muffled cries. Then, smiling, they turned and went out and back down the tunnel, just as the teacher arrived.

"Ready, children?" She glanced at her watch.

"Yes!" said everyone.

"Are we all here?"

"Yes!"

The rain slackened still more.

They crowded to the huge door.

The rain stopped.

It was as if, in the midst of a film concerning an avalanche, a tornado, a hurricane, a volcanic eruption, something had, first, gone wrong with the sound apparatus, thus muffling and finally cutting off all noise, all of the blasts and repercussions and thunders, and then, second, ripped the film from the projector and inserted in its place a peaceful tropical slide which did not move or tremor. The world ground to a standstill.

The silence was so immense and unbelievable that you felt your ears had been stuffed or you had lost your hearing altogether. The children put their hands to their ears. They stood apart. The door slid back and the smell of the silent, waiting world came in to them.

The sun came out.

It was the color of flaming bronze and it was very large.

And the sky around it was a blazing blue tile color. And the jungle burned with sunlight as the children, released from their spell, rushed out, yelling, into the springtime.

"Now, don't go too far," called the teacher after them.

"You've only one hour, you know. You wouldn't want to get caught out!"

But they were running and turning their faces up to the sky and feeling the sun on their cheeks like a warm iron; they were taking off their jackets and letting the sun burn their arms.

"Oh, it's better than sun lamps, isn't it?"

"Much, much better!"

They stopped running and stood in the great jungle that covered Venus, that grew and never stopped growing, tumultuously, even as you watched it. It was a nest of octopuses, clustering up great arms of fleshlike weed, wavering, flowering in this brief spring. It was the color of rubber and ash, this jungle, from the many years without sun. It was the color of stones and white cheeses and ink, and it was the color of the moon.

The children lay out, laughing, on the jungle mattress, and heard it sigh and squeak under them, resilient and alive. They ran among the trees, they slipped and fell, they pushed each other, they played hide-and-seek and tag; but most of all they squinted at the sun until tears ran down their faces, they put their hands up to that yellowness and that amazing blueness and they breathed of the fresh, fresh air and listened and listened to the silence which suspended them in a blessed sea of no sound and no motion. They looked at everything and savored everything. Then, wildly, like animals escaped from their caves, they ran and ran in shouting circles. They ran for an hour and did not stop running.

And then—

In the midst of their running one of the girls wailed.

Everyone stopped.

The girl, standing in the open, held out her hand.

"Oh, look, look," she said trembling.

They came slowly to look at her opened palm.

In the center of it, cupped and huge, was a single raindrop.

She began to cry, looking at it.

They glanced quickly at the sky.

"Oh. Oh."

A few cold drops fell on their noses and their cheeks and their mouths. The sun faded behind a stir of mist. A wind blew cool around them. They turned and started to walk back toward the underground house, their hands at their sides, their smiles vanishing away.

A boom of thunder startled them and like leaves before a new hurricane, they tumbled upon each other and ran. Lightning struck ten miles away, five miles away, a mile, a half mile. The sky darkened into midnight in a flash.

They stood in the doorway of the underground for a moment until it was raining hard. Then they closed the door and heard the gigantic sound of the rain falling in tons and avalanches, everywhere and forever.

"Will it be seven more years?"

"Yes. Seven."

Then one of them gave a little cry.

"Margot!"

"What?"

"She's still in the closet where we locked her."

"Margot."

They stood as if someone had driven them, like so many stakes, into the floor. They looked at each other and then looked away. They glanced out at the world that was raining now and raining and raining steadily. They could not meet each other's glances. Their faces were solemn and pale. They looked at their hands and feet, their faces down.

"Margot."

One of the girls said, "Well . . . ?"

No one moved.

"Go on," whispered the girl.

They walked slowly down the hall in the sound of cold rain.

They turned through the doorway to the room in the sound of the storm and thunder, lightning on their faces, blue and terrible. They walked over to the closet door slowly and stood by it.

Behind the closet door was only silence.

They unlocked the door, even more slowly, and let Margot out. ❖

❊ What was your initial response to what happened in the story? Did you expect it to turn out the way it did?

_____

_____

_____

❊ Now return to the story. Underline any information you find about Margot and William. Make inferences about the characters, and then write a dialogue between Margot and William. What would they say to each other after Margot comes out of the closet?

_____

_____

_____

_____

_____

_____

_____

Making inferences about the characters can help you understand and remember the story.

The **main idea** is the central focus of a piece of nonfiction. It is the most important thing the writer wants you to know. Interacting with the text by finding the main idea is key to understanding what you read.

You can usually discover the main idea by first identifying the **subject** of the writing (the person, place, or thing the author is writing about) and then figuring out what the author has to say about the subject. You can use this equation to figure out the main idea:

[subject] + [what the author says about the subject] = main idea

As you read the first part of the essay, make notes about the subject. Underline words and phrases that give you clues about the main idea.

"Hearing the Sweetest Songs" by Nicolette Toussaint

Response Notes

Every year when I was a child, a man brought a big, black, squeaking machine to school. When he discovered I couldn't hear all his peeps and squeaks, he would get very excited. The nurse would draw a chart with a deep canyon in it. Then I would listen to the squeaks two or three times, while the adults—who were all acting very, very nice—would watch me raise my hand. Sometimes I couldn't tell whether I heard the squeaks or just imagined them, but I liked being the center of attention.

My parents said I lost my hearing to pneumonia as a baby, but I knew I hadn't lost anything. None of my parts had dropped off. Nothing had changed: if I wanted to listen to Beethoven, I could put my head between the speakers and turn the dial up to 7. I could hear jets at the airport a block away. I could hear my mom when she was in the same room—if I wanted to. I could even hear my cat purr if I put my good ear right on top of him.

I wasn't aware of not hearing until I began to wear a hearing aid at the age of 30. It shattered my peace: shoes creaking, papers crackling, pencils tapping, phones ringing, refrigerators humming, people cracking knuckles, clearing throats and blowing noses! Cars, bikes, dogs, cats, kids all seemed to appear from nowhere and fly right at me.

I was constantly startled, unnerved, agitated—exhausted. I felt as though inquisitorial Nazis in an old World War II film were burning the side of my head with a merciless white spotlight. Under that onslaught, I had to break down and confess: I couldn't hear. Suddenly, I began to discover many things I couldn't do.

I couldn't identify sounds. One afternoon, while lying on my side watching a football game on TV, I kept hearing a noise that sounded like my cat playing with a flexible-spring doorstop. I checked, but the cat was asleep. Finally, I happened to lift my head as the noise occurred. Heard through my good ear, the metallic buzz turned out to be the referee's whistle. I couldn't tell where sounds came from. I couldn't find my phone under the blizzard of papers on my desk. The more it rang, the deeper I dug. I shoveled mounds of paper onto the floor and finally had to track it down by following the cord from the wall.

When I lived alone, I felt helpless because I couldn't hear alarm clocks, vulnerable because I couldn't hear the front door open and frightened because I wouldn't hear a burglar until it was too late.

Then one day I missed a job interview because of the phone. I had gotten off the subway twenty minutes early, eager and dressed to the nines. But the address I had written down didn't exist! I must have misheard it. I searched the street, becoming overheated, late and frantic, knowing that if I confessed that I couldn't hear on the phone, I would make my odds of getting hired even worse.

For the first time, I felt unequal, disadvantaged, and disabled. Now that I had something to compare, I knew that I had lost something; not just my hearing, but my independence and my sense of wholeness. I had always hated to be seen as inferior, so I never mentioned my lack of hearing. Unlike a wheelchair or a white cane, my disability doesn't announce itself. For most of my life, I chose to pass as abled, and I thought I did it quite well. ❖

✳ Look at your **Response Notes** and markings on the text. What seems to be the most important idea that Toussaint wants you to understand? State it in your own words using the equation on page 33.

_____ + _____ = _____
       subject   what the author   main idea

                                       says about the subject

✳ Find the sentence in the essay that best expresses the author's main idea and underline it.

✳ Now it's your turn. When have you felt "unequal, disabled, [or] disadvantaged"? Write about one incident. Explain what happened and how you felt. Before you begin, you might want to talk with a partner to help you focus on your main idea. Together, create a main idea equation for your writing

_____ + _____ = _____

subject   what I think   main idea

about the subject

Use the space below to describe your incident.

_____

_____

_____

_____

_____

_____

_____

_____

_____

_____

_____

_____

_____

_____

_____

_____

_____

_____

_____

_____

_____

Recognizing the main idea helps you understand what the author thinks is most important about a subject.

DETERMINING THE AUTHOR'S PURPOSE

Strategic readers look for the **author's purpose** to better understand the author's ideas. Authors write for a variety of reasons, including the following: to entertain, to inform or teach, to persuade or argue, and to express personal thoughts and feelings. Sometimes an author will combine purposes in a piece of writing, such as informing you about a situation and persuading you to do something about it. You can determine an author's purpose or purposes by paying attention to what he or she emphasizes in the writing.

Finish reading the essay "Hearing the Sweetest Songs" to get a sense of what the author wants you to understand. In the **Response Notes,** write your impressions—what puzzles you, what you relate to, and what you like.

Response Notes

"Hearing the Sweetest Songs" by Nicolette Toussaint
(continued)

But after I got the hearing aid, a business friend said, "You know, Nicolette, you think you get away with not hearing, but you don't. Sometimes in meetings you answer the wrong question. People don't know you can't hear, so they think you're daydreaming, eccentric, stupid—or just plain rude. It would be better to just tell them."

I wondered about that then, and I still do. If I tell, I risk being seen as unable rather than disabled. Sometimes, when I say I can't hear, the waiter will turn to my companion and say, "What does she want?" as though I have lost my power of speech.

If I tell, people may see only my disability. Once someone is labeled "deaf," "crippled," "mute" or "aged," that's too often all they are. I'm a writer, a painter, a slapdash housekeeper, a gardener who grows wondrous roses; my hearing is just part of the whole. It's a tender part, and you should handle it with care. But like most people with a disability, I don't mind if you ask about it.

In fact, you should ask, because it's an important part of me, something my friends see as part of my character. My friend Anne always rests a hand on my elbow in parking lots, since several times, drivers who assume that I hear them have nearly run me over. When I hold my head at a certain angle, my husband, Mason, will say "It's a plane" or "It's a siren." And my mother loves to laugh about the things I thought I heard: last week I was told that "the Minotaurs in the garden are getting out of hand." I imagined capering bullmen and I was disappointed to learn that all we had in the garden were overgrown "baby tears."

Not hearing can be funny, or frustrating. And once in a while, it can be the cause of something truly transcendent. One morning at the shore I was listening to the ocean when Mason said, "Hear the bird?" What bird? I listened hard until I heard a faint, unbirdlike, croaking sound. If he hadn't mentioned it, I would never have noticed it. As I listened, slowly I began to hear—or perhaps imagine—a distant song. Did I really hear it? Or just hear in my heart what he shared with me? I don't care. Songs imagined are as sweet as songs heard, and songs shared are sweeter still.

That sharing is what I want for all of us. We're all just temporarily abled, and every one of us, if we live long enough, will become disabled in some way. Those of us who have gotten there first can tell you how to cope with phones and alarm clocks. About ways of holding a book, opening a door and leaning on a crutch all at the same time. And what it's like to give up in despair on Thursday, then begin all over again on Friday, because there's no other choice—and because the roses are beginning to bud in the garden.

These are conversations we all should have, and it's not that hard to begin. Just let me see your lips when you speak. Stay in the same room. Don't shout. And ask what you want to know. ❖

✳ **Discuss this selection with a partner or small group and compare your impressions. What do you think Toussaint wants you to understand?**

✳ What do you think Toussaint's purpose is? In the center of the web, write your answer. Write the details that she emphasizes to support her purpose in the other ovals.

Toussaint's purpose

Authors select and emphasize details that support their purposes for writing.

REFLECTING 10 LESSON

When you take time to think about what you read, you are **reflecting.** This strategy can be used with any type of writing. It is especially useful when you are reading something new or difficult to understand. One way to interact with the text through reflection is to connect your experiences to those in the writing.

Look again at the two selections in this unit. They both dealt with differences. In "All Summer in a Day" (page 26), Margot felt separated from the other children. In "Hearing the Sweetest Songs" (page 33), Toussaint discussed how having a hearing impairment made her different. Choose one of the selections. Write a paragraph to answer each of the following questions.

- What relevant connections can you make between the experiences in the selection and your experience?

✳ What do you learn by making connections?

Reflecting on what you read by making connections to your experience helps you understand new or difficult material.

© GREAT SOURCE. COPYING IS PROHIBITED.

Making Connections

Your life is like a story because it has the same basic elements that are developed in most stories: people, places, and events. Think how the basic elements of a story are present in one of your strongest memories. Who were the people involved? Where were you? What events created joy, conflict, or suspense? What lessons did you learn? A good author will skillfully blend these basic elements to create a story. A good reader understands the elements and appreciates how they work together.

In this unit, you'll learn about five of the basic **elements of a story:**

- setting
- character
- point of view
- story line and plot
- theme

You'll also discover how authors use and combine these elements to create stories.

SETTING

Setting is the time and place of a story, when and where the action occurs. Think about a favorite memory. Could it have taken place anywhere else but where it did?

In some stories, the setting is one of the most important elements. It's hard to imagine Peter Pan without Neverland or Batman without Gotham City. In other stories you might not focus on the setting, although it's there if you look for it.

Read this short passage from Natalie Babbitt's novel *The Search for Delicious*. Circle any words or phrases that relate to the setting. Use your **Response Notes** to describe when and where the story takes place.

from The Search for Delicious by Natalie Babbitt

Response Notes

There was a time once when the earth was still very young, a time some call the oldest days. This was long before there were any people about to dig parts of it up and cut parts of it off. People came along much later, building their towns and castles (which nearly always fell down after a while) and plaguing each other with quarrels and supper parties. The creatures who lived on the earth in that early time stayed each in his own place and kept it beautiful. There were dwarfs in the (mountains,) woldwellers in the (forest,) mermaids in the (lakes,) and, of course, winds in the air. ✧

Sounds like the country.

Next, read the following passage from Madeleine L'Engle's novel *A Wrinkle in Time*. Circle any words or phrases that relate to *setting*. Use your **Response Notes** to describe when and where you think the story takes place.

from A Wrinkle in Time by Madeleine L'Engle

"But where am I?" Meg asked breathlessly, relieved to hear that her voice was now coming out of her in more or less a normal way.

She looked around rather wildly. They were standing in a sunlit field, and that air about them was moving with the delicious fragrance that comes only on the rarest of spring days when the sun's touch is gentle and the apple blossoms are just beginning to unfold. She pushed her glasses up on her nose to reassure herself that what she was seeing was real.

They had left the silver glint of a biting autumn evening; and now around them everything was golden with light. The grasses of the field were a tender new green, and scattered about were tiny, multicolored flowers. Meg turned slowly to face a mountain reaching so high into the sky that its peak was lost in a crown of puffy white clouds. From the trees at the base of the mountain came a sudden singing of birds. There was an air of such ineffable peace and joy all around her that her heart's wild thumping slowed. ✢

✳ With a partner, discuss when and where these stories take place. Write the type of story each setting might introduce.

_____

_____

✳ You have been hired to illustrate the cover for either Babbitt's or L'Engle's novel. Imagine what scene you would draw to show the setting. Choose the novel that is most interesting to you. Use colored pencils, markers, crayons, or pastels to create the cover in the space below.

The time and place of the setting can influence a story.

12 CHARACTERS

Characters are the people, animals, and even imaginary creatures that "live" through the events in a story. Some characters are memorable because of how the author describes them—how they look, act, or talk. Some authors make their characters interesting by giving details about what the characters think and feel. The way an author develops the character is called **characterization**. The better you know a character, the more you will be able to understand the character and the story.

Read the following excerpt from the novel *Danny the Champion of the World*. According to the narrator, Danny, what makes his father special? As you read, list details in your **Response Notes** that characterize, or describe, his father.

from Danny the Champion of the World by Roald Dahl

Response Notes

You might think, if you don't know him well, that he was a stern and serious man. He wasn't. He was actually a wildly funny person. What made him appear so serious was the fact that he never smiled with his mouth. He did it all with his eyes. He had brilliant blue eyes and when he thought of something funny, his eyes would flash and, if you looked carefully, you could actually see a tiny little golden spark dancing in the middle of each eye. But the mouth never moved.

I was glad my father was an eye-smiler. It meant he never gave me a fake smile because it's impossible to make your eyes twinkle if you aren't feeling twinkly yourself. A mouth-smile is different. You can fake a mouth-smile any time you want, simply by moving your lips. I've also learned that a real mouth-smile always has an eye-smile to go with it. So watch out, I say, when someone smiles at you with his mouth but his eyes stay the same. It's sure to be a phony.

My father was not what you would call an educated man. I doubt he had read twenty books in his life. But he was a marvelous storyteller. He used to make up a bedtime story for me every single night, and the best ones were turned into serials and went on for many nights running.

One of them, which must have gone on for at least fifty nights, was about an enormous fellow called "The Big Friendly Giant," or "The BFG" for short. The BFG was three times as tall as an ordinary man and his hands were as big as wheelbarrows. He lived in a vast underground cavern not far from our filling station and he only came out into the open when it was dark. Inside the cavern he had a powder factory where he made more than one hundred different kinds of magic powder.

"The Big Friendly Giant makes his magic powders out of the dreams that children dream when they are asleep," he said.

"How?" I asked. "Tell me how, dad."

"Dreams, my love, are very mysterious things. They float around in the night air like little clouds, searching for sleeping people."

"Can you see them?" I asked.

"Nobody can see them."

"Then how does The Big Friendly Giant catch them?"

"Ah," my father said, "that is the interesting part. A dream, you see, as it goes drifting through the night air, makes a tiny little buzzing-humming sound, a sound so soft and low it is impossible for ordinary people to hear it. But The BFG can hear it easily. His sense of hearing is absolutely fantastic."

I loved the intent look on my father's face when he was telling a story. His face was pale and still and distant, unconscious of everything around him.

"The BFG," he said, "can hear the tread of a ladybug's footsteps as she walks across a leaf. He can hear the whisperings of ants as they scurry around in the soil talking to one another. He can hear the sudden shrill cry of pain a tree gives out when a woodman cuts into it with an ax. Ah yes, my darling, there is a whole world of sound around us that we cannot hear because our ears are simply not sensitive enough."

"What happens when he catches the dreams?" I asked.

"He imprisons them in glass bottles and screws the tops down tight," my father said. "He has thousands of these bottles in his cave."

"Does he catch bad dreams as well as good ones?"

"Yes," my father said. "He catches both. But he only uses the good ones in his powders."

"What does he do with the bad ones?"

"He explodes them."

It is impossible to tell you how much I loved my father. When he was sitting close to me on my bunk I would reach out and slide my hand into his, and then he would fold his long fingers around my fist, holding it tight. ❖

✳ **List three words or phrases that best describe Danny's father.**

_____

_____

_____

_____

_____

A Character Map is a way to organize information about characters. Create a Character Map for Danny's father. Record what you have
learned about Danny's father in the space provided. The prompts on
the map show the types of information to include.

CHARACTER MAP

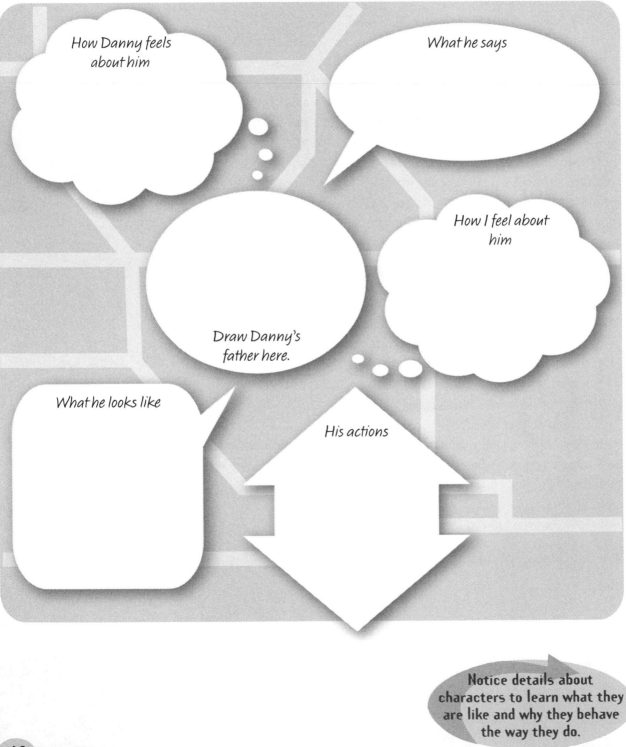

How Danny feels
about him

What he says

How I feel about
him

Draw Danny's
father here.

What he looks like

His actions

Notice details about
characters to learn what they
are like and why they behave
the way they do.

Your perspective, or **point of view**, is how you see an event. If someone else were to tell part of your life story, think how different the perspective would be. How might a close friend tell the story of a moment that was embarrassing to you? What would be different about how you told the story and how your friend told the story?

In order to understand a story's point of view, you must first determine who the narrator is and what the narrator knows. Notice whether the narrator is a character in the story or someone outside the story who describes what takes place.

Read another excerpt from *Danny the Champion of the World*. The narrator is Danny, who is a character in the story. The way Danny tells the story will give you clues to his character. Use your **Response Notes** to jot down things you learn about Danny from his description of his father and the events of the day. What type of person do you think Danny is?

from **Danny the Champion of the World** by Roald Dahl

And so life went on. The world I lived in consisted only of the filling station, the workshop, the caravan, the school, and of course the woods and meadows and streams in the countryside around. But I was never bored. It was impossible to be bored in my father's company. He was too sparky a man for that. Plots and plans and new ideas came flying off him like sparks from a grindstone.

"There's a good wind today," he said one Saturday morning. "Just right for flying a kite. Let's make a kite, Danny."

So we made a kite. He showed me how to splice four thin sticks together in the shape of a star, with two more sticks across the middle to brace it. Then we cut up an old blue shirt of his and stretched that material across the framework of the kite. We added a long tail made of thread, with little leftover pieces of the shirt tied at intervals along it. We found a ball of string in the workshop, and he showed me how to attach the string to the framework so that the kite would be properly balanced in flight.

Together we walked to the top of the hill behind the filling station to release the kite. I found it hard to believe that this object, made only from a few sticks and a piece of old shirt, would actually fly. I held the string while my father held the kite, and the moment he let it go, it caught the wind and soared upward like a huge blue bird.

"Let out some more, Danny!" he cried. "Go on! As much as you like!"

Higher and higher soared the kite. Soon it was just a small blue dot dancing in the sky miles above my head, and it was thrilling to stand there

holding on to something that was so far away and so very much alive. This faraway thing was tugging and struggling on the end of line like a big fish.

"Let's walk it back to the caravan," my father said.

So we walked down the hill again with me holding the string and the kite still pulling fiercely on the other end. When we came to the caravan we were careful not to get the string tangled in the apple tree and we brought it all the way around to the front steps.

"Tie it to the steps," my father said.

"Will it still stay up?" I asked.

"It will if the wind doesn't drop," he said.

The wind didn't drop. And I will tell you something amazing. That kite stayed up there all through the night, and at breakfast time next morning the small blue dot was still dancing and swooping in the sky. After breakfast I hauled it down and hung it carefully against a wall in the workshop for another day. ✤

✳ Write what you learned about Danny by the way he narrates the story of the kite-flying incident.

_____
_____
_____

✳ Like Danny, you have stories to tell. Think of an experience that was important to you. Write a quick draft that describes the experience. Remember, the way you tell the story reveals the type of person you are.

_____
_____
_____
_____
_____
_____
_____
_____

Determine who is telling the story. Look for clues about what type of person the narrator is.

14 LESSON

The **story line** is the sequence of events in the order they are told in a story. A story line is a timeline. You can list everything that happened in the order it appears in the story. Take a look at the events on the story line below.

Band practice was cancelled.	A boy broke his arm.	The band took 3rd place.	A rainstorm created a sink-hole in a field.
#1	#2	#3	#4

Just listing the events in the order in which they appear in the story doesn't tell a story. Something is missing. One way to examine what's missing is to see how the events are presented in the story. As you read the short story "There's No Sweet Revenge," circle each of the events listed above when you come across it. In your **Response Notes,** explain what you think each event contributes to the story.

"There's No Sweet Revenge" by Ruth Vinz

Band practice is cancelled and we all jump up and down like there is no tomorrow. My first thought is that Jerry and I have time to go for ice cream before heading home. No one expects us for at least an hour. If I go home my mom will nag me about my homework. We all head off at full steam, running to our lockers. We've been practicing for months. We want to keep our title as Jefferson Middle School #1 Best Band in the State. But no practice is a higher priority. At least, for now.

As we get to our lockers, we hear the new kid in the trumpet section yelling his head off. He annoys me anyway because he thinks he's the best trumpet player we've got. I'm thinking about him for about one second before I hear the sound of voices. "Who? Who? What happened?" It's Mr. Zino, our principal, sounding as excited as ever. He chirps when he talks. We yell, "hey, hurry up" to our friends and take off running before Zino can stop us. We rule the afternoon.

It isn't until the next day we learn what happened. Our band teacher stands in the doorway, looking like he swallowed a pickle. The whole band is chirping like Zino, passing around information. Seems that the new kid broke his arm. Can't play trumpet for at least six weeks. That means I lead the section. I'm having little grinning fits about that. Until I think about the competition in three days.

As it turns out, we don't take last place but not the top one either. We place 3rd and everybody is quiet. The new kid stands on the sidelines jumping up and down like a grasshopper and annoying me all over again. That red cast on his

Response Notes

Response Notes

arm pokes into Melanie Brooks as he pitches a fit about our losing first place. He looks up. And then for no reason that I can recall, I stretch back in my mind to imagine the moment he fell in that sinkhole, the one that opened up when the heavy rains came. And, I'm almost glad he did. And, I'm almost glad we didn't take first with him as section leader. And I'm almost, well, feeling the sting in my eyes that brings tears. But instead, I look straight at him and flash a big smile, teeth and all. "Next time," I yell. "come on over to my house if you want. We're having a celebration party." And I march off just like that. ✣

A story line is the sequence of events as they occur in the story. The **plot** emphasizes how events and characters are connected.

- Think about what each of the four events on the story line contributes to the plot of the story. Discuss with a partner how each part forms a connection to other parts of the story.

A *plot* can be divided into five parts: *exposition, rising action, climax, falling action,* and *resolution.*

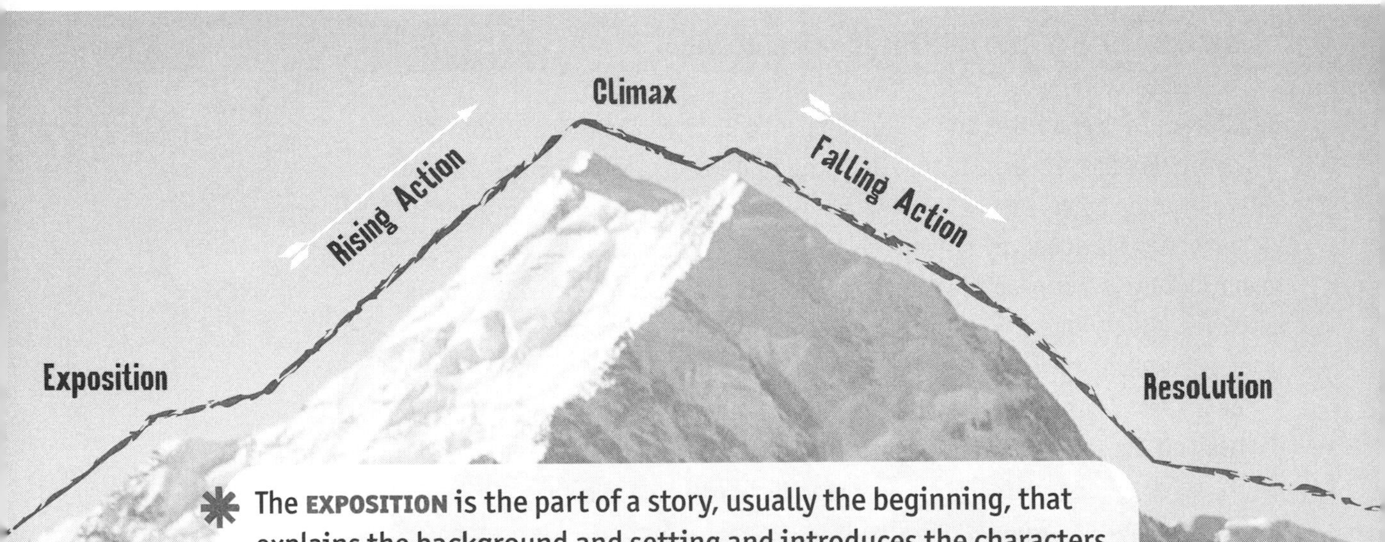

- The **EXPOSITION** is the part of a story, usually the beginning, that explains the background and setting and introduces the characters.
- The **RISING ACTION** is the central part of a story during which various problems arise, leading up to the climax.
- The **CLIMAX** is the highest point, or the turning point, in the action of a story. The climax causes the action of the story to change.
- The **FALLING ACTION** follows the climax or turning point. It contains the action or dialogue necessary to lead the story to a resolution or ending.
- The **RESOLUTION** is the end of a story—that part in which the problems are resolved or the story gets "wrapped up."

Now that you have an idea about how a plot works, read the first part of the story "Abuela Invents the Zero," by Judith Ortiz Cofer. In your **Response Notes,** keep track of the major events that may be important in the story's plot.

"Abuela Invents the Zero" by Judith Ortiz Cofer

Response Notes

"You made me feel like a zero, like a nothing," she says in Spanish, *un cero, nada.* She is trembling, an angry little old woman lost in a heavy winter coat that belongs to my mother. And I end up being sent to my room, like I was a child, to think about my grandmother's idea of math.

It all began with Abuela coming up from the Island for a visit—her first time in the United States. My mother and father paid her way here so that she wouldn't die without seeing snow, though if you asked me, and nobody has, the dirty slush in this city is not worth the price of a ticket. But I guess she deserves some kind of award for having had ten kids and survived to tell about it. My mother is the youngest of the bunch. Right up to the time when we're supposed to pick up that old lady at the airport, my mother is telling me stories about how hard times were for *la familia* on *la isla,* and how *la abuela* worked night and day to support them after their father died of a heart attack. I'd die of a heart attack too if I had a troop like that to support. Anyway, I had seen her only three or four times in my entire life, whenever we would go for somebody's funeral. I was born here and I have lived in this building all my life. But when Mami says, "Connie, please be nice to Abuela. She doesn't have too many years left. Do you promise me, Constancia?"—when she uses my full name, I know she means business. So I say, "Sure." Why wouldn't I be nice? I'm not a monster, after all.

So we go to Kennedy to get la abuela and she is the last to come out of the airplane, on the arm of the cabin attendant, all wrapped up in a black shawl. He hands her over to my parents like she was a package sent airmail. It is January, two feet of snow on the ground, and she's wearing a shawl over a thin black dress. That's just the start.

Once home, she refuses to let my mother buy her a coat because it's a waste of money for the two weeks she'll be in *el Polo Norte,* as she calls New Jersey, the North Pole. So since she's only four feet eleven inches tall, she walks around in my mother's big black coat looking ridiculous. I try to walk far behind them in public so that no one will think we're together. I plan to stay very busy the whole time she's with us so that I won't be asked to take her anywhere, but my plan is ruined when my mother comes down with the flu and Abuela absolutely has to attend Sunday mass or her soul will be eternally damned. She's more Catholic than the Pope. My father decides that he should stay home with my mother and that I should escort la abuela to church. He tells me this on Saturday night as I'm getting ready to go out to the mall with my friends.

Response Notes

"No way," I say.

I go for the car keys on the kitchen table: he usually leaves them there for me on Friday and Saturday nights. He beats me to them.

"No way," he says pocketing them and grinning at me.

Needless to say, we come to a compromise very quickly. I do have a responsibility to Sandra and Anita, who don't drive yet. There is a Harley-Davidson fashion show at Brookline Square that we *cannot* miss.

"The mass in Spanish is at ten sharp tomorrow morning, *entiendes?*" My father is dangling the car keys in front of my nose and pulling them back when I try to reach for them. He's really enjoying himself.

Fill in as much of the Plot Diagram as you can. You won't have everything filled in yet, nor will the order of events be clear until you've read the entire story.

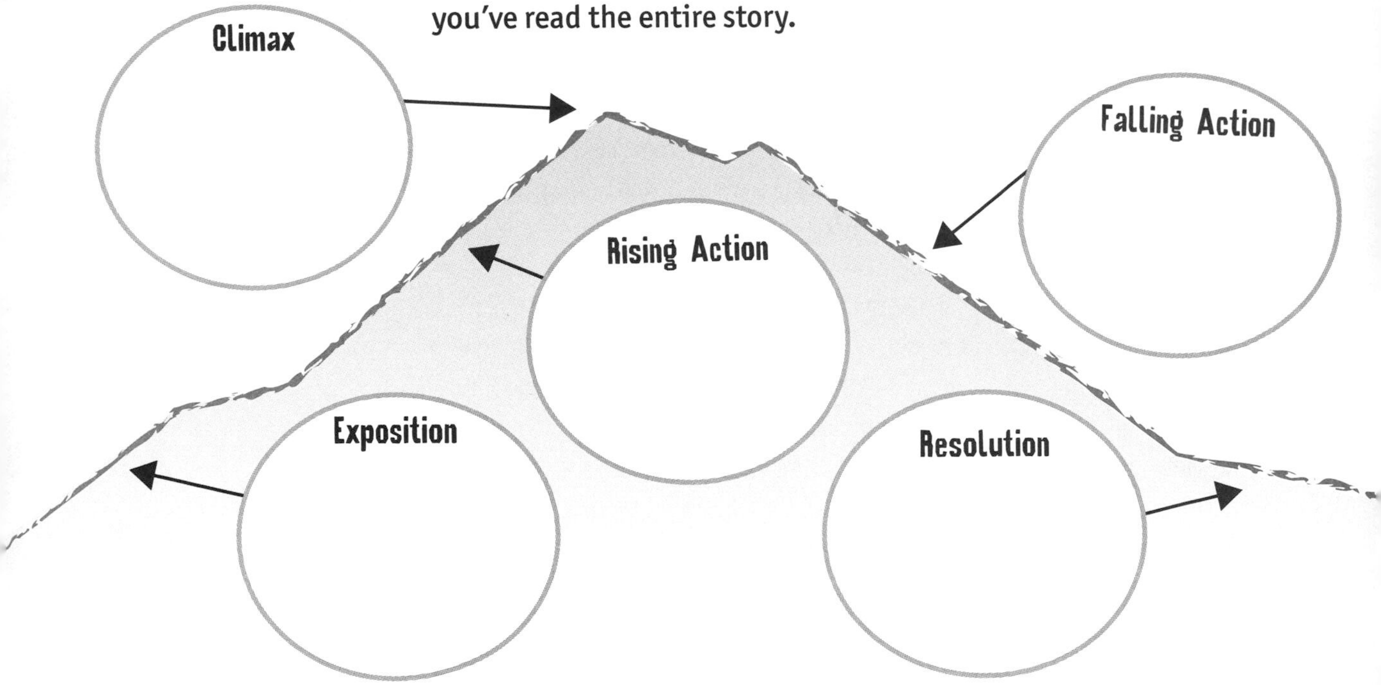

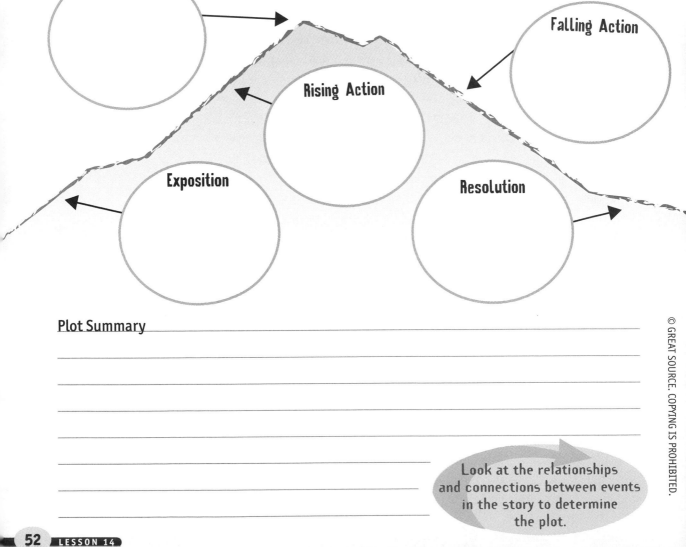

Plot Summary

Look at the relationships and connections between events in the story to determine the plot.

A story's **theme** is its central idea. The theme is the statement or message from the author. Often you can connect a story's plot and theme to your own life. Ask yourself: What does this author want me to think or understand from the story? Sometimes the author will make the theme obvious by stating the idea directly. Other times you'll need to make inferences, or reasonable guesses, about the theme from what the author says and the way the plot is constructed.

Continue reading "Abuela Invents the Zero" by Judith Ortiz Cofer. Use your **Response Notes** to note major events and to tie these to the lessons Cofer seems to be emphasizing.

"Abuela Invents the Zero" by Judith Ortiz Cofer
(continued)

Response Notes

"I understand. Ten o'clock. I'm out of here." I pry his fingers off the key ring. He knows that I'm late, so he makes it just a little difficult. Then he laughs. I run out of our apartment before he changes his mind. I have no idea what I'm getting myself into.

Sunday morning I have to walk two blocks on dirty snow to retrieve the car. I warm it up for Abuela as instructed by my parents, and drive it to the front of our building. My father walks her by the hand in baby steps on the slippery snow. The sight of her little head with a bun on top of it sticking out of that huge coat make me want to run back into my room and get under the covers. I just hope that nobody I know sees us together. I'm dreaming, of course. The mass is packed with people from our block. It's a holy day of obligation and everyone I ever met is there.

I have to help her climb the steps, and she stops to take a deep breath after each one, then I lead her down the aisle so that everybody can see me with my bizarre grandmother. If I were a good Catholic, I'm sure I'd get some purgatory time taken off for my sacrifice. She is walking as slow as Captain Cousteau exploring the bottom of the sea, looking around, taking her sweet time. Finally she chooses a pew, but she wants to sit in the *other* end. It's like she had a spot picked out for some unknown reason, and although it's the most inconvenient seat in the house, that's where she has to sit. So we squeeze by all the people already sitting there, saying, "Excuse me, please, *con permiso,* pardon me," getting annoyed looks the whole way. By the time we settle in, I'm drenched in sweat. I keep my head down like I'm praying so as not to see or be seen. She is praying loud, in Spanish, and singing hymns at the top of her creaky voice.

I ignore her when she gets up with a hundred other people to go take communion. I'm actually praying hard now—that this will all be over soon.

But the next time I look up, I see a black coat dragging around and around the church, stopping here and there so a little gray head can peek out like a periscope on a submarine. There are giggles in the church, and even the priest has frozen in the middle of a blessing, his hands above his head like he is about to lead the congregation in a set of jumping jacks.

I realize to my horror that my grandmother is lost. She can't find her way back to the pew. I am so embarrassed that even though the woman next to me is shooting daggers at me with her eyes, I just can't move to go get her. I put my hands over my face like I'm praying, but it's really to hide my burning cheeks. I would like for her to disappear. I just know that on Monday my friends, and my enemies, in the barrio will have a lot of senile-grandmother jokes to tell in front of me. I am frozen to my seat. So the same woman who wants me dead on the spot does it for me. She makes a big deal out of getting up and hurrying to get Abuela.

The rest of the mass is a blur. All I know is that my grandmother kneels the whole time with *her* hands over her face. She doesn't speak to me on the way home, and she doesn't let me help her walk, even though she almost falls a couple of times.

When we get to the apartment, my parents are at the kitchen table, where my mother is trying to eat some soup. They can see right away that something is wrong. Then Abuela points her finger at me like a judge passing a sentence on a criminal. She says in Spanish, "You made me feel like a zero, like a nothing." Then she goes to her room.

I try to explain what happened. "I don't understand why she's so upset. She just got lost and wandered around for a while," I tell them. But it sounds lame, even to my own ears. My mother gives me a look that makes me cringe and goes in to Abuela's room to get her version of the story. She comes out with tears in her eyes.

"Your grandmother says to tell you that of all the hurtful things you can do to a person, the worst is to make them feel as if they are worth nothing."

I can feel myself shrinking right there in front of her. But I can't bring myself to tell my mother that I think I understand how I made Abuela feel. I might be sent into the old lady's room to apologize, and it's not easy to admit you've been a jerk—at least, not right away with everybody watching. So I just sit there not saying anything.

My mother looks at me for a long time, like she feels sorry for me. Then she says, "You should know, Constancia, that if it wasn't for this old woman whose existence you don't seem to value, you and I would not be here."

That's when *I'm* sent to *my* room to consider a number I hadn't thought much about—until today. ❖

※ First, add events from this part of the story to the Plot Diagram on page 52. Share your thinking with a partner. Discuss how you think the events are related. Then write a summary of the plot.

※ In the Theme Organizer, organize your thinking about the important messages from the story.

THEME ORGANIZER

1. Important Quotes What I Think About This

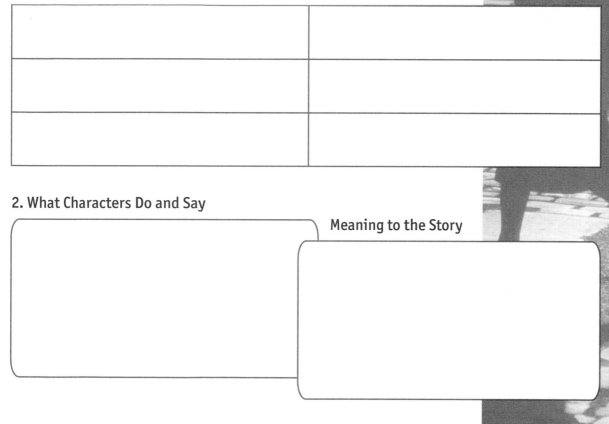

2. What Characters Do and Say

Meaning to the Story

3. Big Ideas **4. Lessons Learned**

Write a paragraph describing what you see as one of the themes of the story. Use your Theme Organizer to provide evidence or use quotes to support your opinions.

_____

_____

_____

_____

_____

_____

_____

_____

Connect this theme to your own life. Describe an experience or situation you've had that relates to the story's theme. What did you learn from your experience?

_____

_____

_____

_____

_____

_____

_____

_____

_____

_____

_____

_____

If you can connect the theme from the story to your own experiences, then you will understand the story better.

Exploring Multiple Perspectives

When you want to buy a new pair of shoes, how do you decide what to buy? You probably look at the shoes your friends are wearing. You might consult your parents. If you want specialized shoes, such as shoes made for soccer players, you might look at ads in a sports magazine. You might even check a website to compare prices and features. The point is that you probably would get more than one opinion, or perspective.

Exploring many perspectives is an important part of your repertoire of skills and strategies. It helps you learn more about a subject. The more you learn, the better able you are to make up your own mind. Sometimes finding out what "really happened" is like putting together a jigsaw puzzle. Each source has some of the information, but you need all of the pieces to **get the big picture.** By reading about the sinking of the *Titanic* in this unit, you will explore perspectives that may or may not agree with each other. You will have to decide what really happened on that cold April night in 1912.

16 ESTABLISHING THE SEQUENCE OF EVENTS

The first step in exploring multiple perspectives is to figure out what happened. You need to know the order, or **sequence**, of events. When you know the sequence of events, you can compare what people say about the event to what you know about it. For example, soon after a disaster occurs, the facts are not always clear. You should know that if you read about a disaster right away, you should question whether the facts are correct. As you can see on the front page of Baltimore's *The Evening Sun,* the first reports about the *Titanic* were not accurate.

As you read the following excerpt, pay attention to the sequence of events. Circle words and phrases that show when events happened.

from **The Titanic** by Richard Wormser

Response Notes

The night was bitter cold. Stars shone like diamonds in the dark sky, but there was no moon. The water was calm, and smooth as glass. High in the crow's nest, two young sailors, Frederick Fleet and Herbert Lee, were watching for icebergs. These men were the "eyes of the ship"—part of the team of lookouts. From their perch above the *Titanic*'s deck, they could gaze far out into the open sea and spot any danger before it seriously threatened the ship. Radar and other electronic scanning devices had not yet been invented, so watching closely was the only way to spot objects in the water. But these lookouts didn't even have a pair of binoculars.

By 11:30 P.M., most passengers were in bed. Fleet and Lee were glad their shift would be over in another 20 minutes. They were numb with cold and their eyes hurt from the strain of trying to see in the dark. Then at 11:39 P.M., Fleet suddenly spied an object which at first seemed small but rapidly increased in size. Within seconds he realized that the *Titanic* was headed straight for an iceberg. He snatched up the telephone and rang the bridge, the officer's control center. As soon as the officer answered, Fleet cried out:

"Iceberg dead ahead!"

The great ship was about to meet her fate.

It only took 37 seconds for the *Titanic* to begin its swing away from the 100-foot-high, 500-foot-deep iceberg in its path. To lookouts Fleet and Lee, that was way too long. It seemed certain that the *Titanic* would crash head-on into the mountain of ice. William Murdoch, the first officer in charge, had already given orders to change the ship's course. A ship as large as the *Titanic*, however, needed time to reposition. Fifteen seconds more and the *Titanic* would have escaped. But time was the one thing the *Titanic* didn't have.

The *Titanic* was about to crash into the iceberg when it suddenly began to swerve out of the iceberg's path. To the officers on the bridge, it seemed that their last-minute attempts to change course had worked. The ship appeared to have only lightly scraped the iceberg. But many passengers and crew below were aware that something much more serious had happened. ❖

✳ What is the sequence of events that Wormser describes? Use the diagram below to show what happened first, what happened next, and so on.

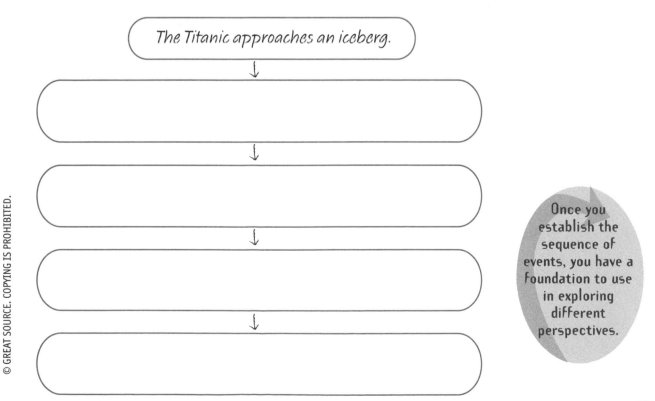

The Titanic approaches an iceberg.

Once you establish the sequence of events, you have a foundation to use in exploring different perspectives.

DETERMINING CAUSE AND EFFECT

Before judging other people's perspectives on an event, you need to understand the event thoroughly. Besides knowing the sequence of events, you need to know the possible **causes and effects**. This means trying to figure out how one event, the cause, brings on related events, the effects. Determining the causes of a disaster, like the sinking of the "unsinkable" *Titanic,* is not easy. Immediately after hitting the iceberg, some passengers and crewmembers knew that something was wrong. But no one knew how devastating the effects would be.

As you read, underline or highlight possible causes of the disaster.

from **The Titanic** by Richard Wormser

Response Notes

Four crew members relaxing in a first-class lounge heard a grinding noise from deep inside the ship. It sounded, one said, as if "a propeller had fallen off." Many first-class passengers felt a shock. To Marguerite Frolicher, a young Swiss woman, it seemed, "as if the ship were landing." Lady Duff Gordon, a dress designer married to a British nobleman, commented that it was as if "someone had run a giant finger along the side of the ship."

On the ship's lower decks, the noise was even louder. Some people in second class were awakened by the jolt. Major Arthur Godfrey Peuchen, a Canadian, thought "a heavy wave" had struck the ship. Mrs. Walter Stephenson, who had lived through the 1906 San Francisco earthquake, thought the shock felt like an earthquake tremor.

Deep within the ship, the men tending the boilers that powered the *Titanic* knew exactly what had happened. In one of the boiler rooms, a tremendous rumbling, scraping sound was heard, followed by a terrifying roar as tons of sea water came crashing into the ship. The whole left side of the ship seemed to collapse suddenly. The men barely escaped with their lives.

In the third-class area, Carl Bohme, a Finnish immigrant, got out of bed to see what was going on and found himself up to his ankles in water. In the mailroom, the water was already covering the knees of the postal workers, who were frantically trying to keep the mail from getting wet.

Most passengers still didn't realize how serious things were. Some third-class passengers had discovered that their deck was covered with ice that had fallen from the iceberg. Some began to have a snowball fight. Soon passengers from every class were picking up pieces of ice. Some even used the ice to cool their drinks. Whatever the problem, they seemed confident that it would soon be solved.

A few passengers, however, were well aware that something was terribly wrong. Lawrence Beasley, a schoolteacher traveling in second class, had started back to his cabin when he noticed that somehow his feet weren't falling in the right place. The stairs were level, but he felt slightly off balance. It was as if the steps were suddenly tilting forward toward the *bow*, the front part of the ship. In fact, they were.

Below the decks was Thomas Andrews, the chief engineer who had supervised the design of the *Titanic*. He was on board to see how the ship would perform on her maiden voyage and whether any adjustments needed to be made. No one knew the *Titanic* better than Andrews. No man, not even Captain Smith, commanded more respect from the crew. Now the ship's officers were anxiously waiting for him to tell them what was happening.

Andrews studied the reports of the damage and then gave Captain Smith the bad news: The rock-hard base of the iceberg had scraped the *Titanic*'s hull below the waterline, gashing some holes in her side and loosening the steel plates that held her together. Water was rushing into the front of the ship. Andrews explained there were 16 water-tight compartments on the ship from bow to stern, the back end of the ship. The ship could float if the first four were filled. But if the fifth compartment, or bulkhead, was filled, the bow would begin to sink so low that water would spill over that bulkhead into the sixth compartment. Because the *Titanic*'s bulkheads were not high enough to prevent this from happening, the spillover would continue from compartment to compartment until the whole ship filled with water and sank.

The *Titanic* was doomed.

"How long have we got?" the captain asked.

"About two hours," Andrews replied.

Smith and Andrews both knew that there were 2,207 passengers and crew on board, but room for only about 1,178 people in the lifeboats. Unless a rescue ship arrived within two hours, more than 1,000 people would drown. There was no time to waste. ❖

✳ **On the diagram below, list some of the causes of the *Titanic* disaster.**

1. _____

2. _____

3. _____

4. _____

✳ Imagine that you are one of the surviving crew members. You have been asked to explain the cause of the disaster. Use your diagram and the Sequence Chart you made in Lesson 16 (page 59) to write your official report.

Official Report ⚓

Prepared By: _____

_____

_____

_____

_____

_____

_____

_____

_____

_____

_____

_____

_____

_____

_____

_____

_____

_____

_____

_____

Recognizing cause-and-effect relationships helps you connect events and ideas.

18 CONSIDERING THE AUTHOR'S CREDIBILITY

How do you know what to believe if you get many perspectives on a subject? Do you know which sources are believable? You cannot believe everything you hear, see, or read. You have to make some judgments. Fortunately, there are guidelines that will help you ask good questions. In this lesson, you will learn what questions to ask when your source is the author.

The selections you read in Lessons 16 and 17 were by Richard Wormser, author of the book *The Titanic*. Unless you have researched him, you may not know whether he is **credible**, or believable. Look at those selections again to complete the Background Check. Briefly note the reason for your answer in the space below each item. Answer as best you can for now, given the information you have.

BACKGROUND CHECK ON AN AUTHOR

☐ What is Richard Wormser's purpose for writing about the *Titanic*?

_____

_____

☐ Why did he tell about people on each level of the ship—passengers in first class, second class, and third class, and crew members in first class and in the boiler room?

_____

_____

_____

☐ Where do you think Richard Wormser got his information?

_____

_____

_____

☐ What is Richard Wormser's background?

_____

_____

_____

✳ Evaluate your conclusions with a partner. If you want to make changes to your answers, make them now.

✳ The next step is to find out more about the author to check your conclusions. The quotations below will give you additional data and perhaps another perspective. Richard Wormser wrote an essay for the reference source *Something About the Author Autobiography Series* (1998). He is also listed in *Contemporary Authors Online* (2004). Read the quotations to make **inferences**, or reasonable guesses, about the author's perspective. Write notes about the information in the spaces around the quotations.

"Richard Wormser is a filmmaker-turned-writer who has published several works of nonfiction for young adult readers on such varied topics as teens at risk, Vietnam, hoboes, railways, American Islam, and even a biography of Allan Pinkerton, the first private investigator in the United States. Wormser's writings generally have a social slant...." (CA)

"In the 1970s and 1980s he continued to make documentary films. By the 1990s, though, he 'found it increasingly difficult to produce his social and political documentaries, and turned to writing instead.'" (CA)

"His first book was so well received that he decided to continue writing for young adults. He wrote, 'Perhaps through my books I can reach an audience that is not yet indifferent to the plight of America's dispossessed—those for whom society seems to have no place.'" (SAAS)

✳ Return to the Background Check on page 64 and revise your answers as necessary.

Good authors do a lot of research to establish the details of their story. There is evidence in the selections that Richard Wormser relied on research, too. One piece of information that was not widely reported right after the disaster was the great differences in who died and who survived. There were lifeboats for only about half the passengers. Look at the chart. Who had the best chances of surviving? How might this relate to the author's purpose for writing *The Titanic*? Note your conclusions below the chart.

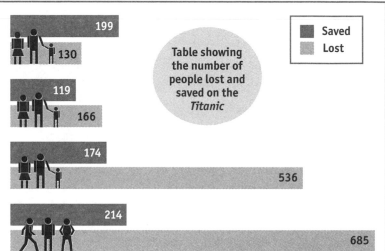

FIRST CLASS Most of the 529 first-class passengers (60%) survived. Most of the survivors were women and children.

SECOND CLASS Slightly fewer than half of the second-class passengers (42%) survived. Most of the survivors were women and children.

THIRD CLASS Only one-quarter (25%) of the third-class passengers survived. More women and children died than survived.

CREW Only 24% of the crew survived. Most of the crew members were men.

199
130
119
166
174
536
214
685

Saved
Lost

Table showing the number of people lost and saved on the *Titanic*

_____

_____

_____

_____

_____

_____

❊ Having checked his background and the facts that he used, would you say that Richard Wormser is a credible source? Explain your thoughts.

_____

_____

_____

_____

Determining the credibility of the author helps you judge the accuracy of what you read.

People at the scene of an event provide important perspectives. But, as readers, we need to remember that they know only what they see and hear. Usually, eyewitnesses do not have the whole picture. As you read this account from a survivor of the *Titanic* disaster, think about what must have been going through his head at the time.

John Thayer, Jr., was 17 when he took a trip to Europe with his parents during spring break. It was his last year in high school, and his father had mapped out John's future in banking. John and his parents were returning to New York on the *Titanic,* traveling first-class. Author Phillip Hoose wrote John's story based on Thayer's 1940 self-published book, *The Sinking of the S. S. Titanic.*

"John Thayer: Becoming a Man Aboard the *Titanic*"
from *We Were There, Too! Young People in U.S. History* by Phillip Hoose

Response Notes

John thought the *Titanic* was astounding. It was really a floating city, four blocks long. You could work out in the gymnasium, take steam baths, or lounge around the pool. There were shops everywhere; even the barber shop sold flags from around the world. As a first-class passenger, John could go anywhere and talk to anyone he wanted to, even the ship's owner.

On the evening of Sunday, April 14, after a dinner conversation with a judge's son named Milton Long, John stepped out onto the deck for some fresh air. He later wrote: "there was no moon and I have never seen the stars shine brighter—they sparkled like cut diamonds . . . It was the kind of night that made one glad to be alive." Yawning, he went down to his stateroom, said good night to his parents, and slipped on his pajamas. He was about to climb into bed when he felt the ship sway very slightly. He wrote, "If I had had a brimful glass of water in my hand not a drop would have been spilled."

The engines stopped and then started up again, and he heard voices outside his door. He put on his overcoat and went to the deck to see what was happening. There were chunks of ice scattered about. A crew member told him they had struck an iceberg. The deck seemed to be tilting a little to the right. A few minutes later John passed the ship's designer, Thomas Andrews, in a corridor. Shaken, Andrews told John he didn't think the ship could float for more than an hour. John's heart began to race. He got dressed, woke his parents, and rushed back to the deck with them to put on life vests and wait for a lifeboat. Milton Long appeared and asked if he could join them.

There was room in the lifeboats for only about half the passengers and crew, so choices had to be made. "Women and children first," people were yelling. John didn't even ask whether he qualified. He could see that much

younger boys than he were being kept from the boats. John knew that on this, maybe the last night of his life, he was considered a man.

At 12:45 A.M. John hugged his mother good-bye, watched her step into a lifeboat, and hurried to the deck on the other side of the boat with his father and Milton. The roar of the steam was deafening. Sailors sent rockets arcing high into the sky to try to attract passing ships. The ship's orchestra was still playing in the background. People were screaming. A surging crowd separated John and Milton from John's father. ✦

✳ What do you think John was thinking while all this was going on? Jot down a few thoughts that might go through someone's head at this point.

✳ What do you think John Thayer does not mention? How differ-ently would someone else on the ship tell about that April evening? Use what you know from your reading to draft a possible eyewitness account.

_____

_____

_____

_____

_____

_____

_____

_____

_____

The author's perspective on a subject determines what information is presented.

20 LESSON

There can be many versions of a story. The viewpoints of people involved in the event will vary, depending on who they are and how they were involved. People studying the event might look at it from the vantage point of their own special interests, such as science or history. Some authors might want to make a point about social injustice or other concerns that they have.

Critical reading requires that you understand and evaluate information. As you read the rest of John Thayer's story, underline or highlight places where you can tell what he's *thinking*. Make notes about what he might be *feeling*.

"John Thayer: Becoming a Man Aboard the *Titanic*"
from *We Were There, Too! Young People in U.S. History* by Phillip Hoose

As one side of the ship continued to list, John and Milton climbed to the upper deck and looked down onto the scene. They had few choices, and none of them was good. They thought about trying to fight their way aboard one of the last two lifeboats, but it looked like those boats would be crushed under the ship anyway. John wanted to slide down a rope, leap into the water, and swim for a lifeboat, but Milton convinced him to wait to jump until the water was close to the deck. The two climbed onto the deck railing as the water drew nearer. "So many thoughts passed so quickly through my mind! I thought of all the good times I had had, and of all the future pleasures I would never enjoy; of my Father and Mother; of my Sisters and Brother . . . It seemed so unnecessary, but we still had a chance, if only we could keep away from the crowd and the suction of the sinking ship."

When the water reached them, John and Milton shook hands and wished each other luck. Milton jumped first, and then John sat on the rail, placed his feet outward, gulped as much air as he could, and leaped. He and the *Titanic* went down at about the same time. "The shock of the water took the breath out of my lungs. Down and down I went, spinning in all directions." John stayed under for at least a minute and then struggled to the surface, popping up just in time to see the great ship split in two. Then the suction dragged him under again. Swimming with all his might, he broke the surface with his hand and grabbed onto an object. It was an overturned lifeboat. Soon twenty-seven other passengers were clinging to it as well.

They hung on in the freezing sea for five hours, singing hymns and trying to keep talking, until they were rescued by sailors from the ocean liner *Carpathia*. John was able to climb the rope ladder by himself. At the top of the ladder, the first face he saw was that of his mother. Hours later, they realized John's father had not survived. ◆

Response Notes

Ruth Becker was only 12 when she boarded the *Titanic*, along with her mother, brother, and sister. As you read, note how this account compares to John Thayer's.

"I Survived the *Titanic*" by Jennifer Kilpatrick

"My mother had just gone to bed when she was awakened by the engines stopping," described Ruth. Their steward told Mrs. Becker to get on deck. "We had to climb five flights of stairs to a room full of women," Ruth recalled. "They were all weeping—in all states of dress and undress. Everyone was frightened—no one knew what would happen to them. But I was never scared. I was only excited. I never for one minute thought we would die." . . .

On deck, the crew fired distress rockets. Mrs. Becker sent Ruth back to their cabin for blankets. Ruth returned to find officers loading women and children in a nearby lifeboat. "One officer grabbed my sister, another carried my brother into the lifeboat and yelled, 'All full!' My mother screamed. They let mother on, but they left me behind.

"My mother yelled at me to take the next lifeboat, and before I knew it, an officer picked me up and dumped me into a boat." . . .

Officers frantically loaded the remaining lifeboats. Passengers prayed. The band played somber hymns. The lights went out as the ship split apart. People screamed and jumped overboard. First the bow went down quietly—then the stern sank. ❖

Ruth was later reunited with her entire family.

✳ Imagine that either Ruth or John had to write an official report about the sinking of the *Titanic* and the rescue of passengers. Draft the beginning of the report. Remember to include only what she or he would know. Capture only the perspective that you would get from one or the other of these two survivors.

Comparing versions of an event helps you piece together the whole picture.

Focusing on Language and Craft

The beauty of poetry lies in how poets shape and use language to create feelings and images. Often, poetry is able to convey more images with fewer words than prose. That's because poets use certain techniques that help them craft ideas into an effective piece of writing.

In this unit, you're going to read a number of poems about different sports. You will also look at the **figurative language** in the poems. You will learn to recognize and use techniques such as the following:

- metaphor
- simile
- imagery
- word choice
- sensory language

Many students are now studying martial arts, such as *tae kwon do, aikido,* and *karate.* Perhaps you are, too. Read this poem by Jane Yolen. Notice that she repeats some words and phrases. Mark those sections. Write what you think about the poem in the **Response Notes.**

Karate Kid by Jane Yolen

I am wind,
I am wall,
I am wave,
I rise, I fall.
I am crane
In lofty flight,
Training that
I need not fight.

I am tiger,
I am tree,
I am flower,
I am knee,
I am elbow,
I am hands
Taught to do
The heart's commands.

Not to bully,
Not to fight
Dragon left
And leopard right.
Wind and wave,
Tree and flower,
Chop.
          Kick.
                    Peace.
                              Power. ❖

PERFORMING THE POEM

Your teacher will organize the class into small groups to read and act out the poem. Each group will organize its own performance.

❊ Here are the instructions for each group:

- ■ Read the poem aloud together, as a group.
- ■ Mark up the poem, underlining any words you don't quite understand.
- ■ Discuss any parts or words you don't understand.
- ■ Talk about words for which you may understand one meaning, but you don't understand how it is used in the poem or story, "Dragon left and leopard right," for example.
- ■ Decide who the speakers and actors will be.
- ■ Decide what actions your group will use to dramatize the poem. Some may speak their lines or strike poses while other students read the lines. You may read lines individually, in pairs, or as a whole group.
- ■ Practice!

❊ Perform the poem for the class. Be attentive while other groups are performing. After the performances, discuss the choices that each group made. Emphasize the effective choices made by each group.

UNDERSTANDING METAPHOR

You may already know the word **metaphor.** Here are a few examples of metaphors that do not come from this poem:

- ■ "I am hawk."
- ■ "Paul Bunyan was a mountain."
- ■ "The moon is a coin."

❊ Work with a partner. Describe how

- ■ a person might be thought of as a hawk
- ■ Paul Bunyan might be considered a mountain
- ■ the moon and a coin are alike

✳ From your discussion, write what the word *metaphor* probably means. Robert Frost said it meant talking about one thing in terms of another, for example, saying the moon is (like) a coin. Notice that the word *like* does not appear in the examples of metaphor on page 73.

_____

_____

✳ What do the three words "I am tiger" make you think or see in your mind? Look for other metaphors in "Karate Kid." Choose one and tell how it helps you think about ideas beyond the words.

_____

_____

_____

_____

Here is a statement of what some people who practice karate believe: "We seek tranquility in the midst of conflict or danger and strive to control our bodies, minds, and emotions to be able to avoid conflict when possible, defend ourselves when necessary, and protect others when able."

✳ Write a paragraph about how you think the poem "Karate Kid" supports that statement. When you write, try to use some of the words in the poem.

_____

_____

_____

_____

_____

_____

_____

A metaphor can help the reader access ideas beyond the literal meaning of the words.

Y ou have already learned something about metaphor. Now you will read a poem that makes very definite comparisons by using a particular kind of **metaphor** called a **simile.**

Read the poem "Skiing" by Bobbi Katz. Put check marks next to lines that help you see images in your mind.

Skiing by Bobbi Katz

Skiing is like being
part of a mountain.
On the early morning run
before the crowds begin,
my skis make
        little blizzards
as they plough
        through untouched powder
to leave fresh tracks
        in the blue-white snow.
My body bends and turns
        to catch each
bend and turn
        the mountain takes;
and I am the mountain
and the mountain is me. ❖

Response Notes

❋ Do a quickdraw of the poem in the space below. Underline the parts of the poem you included in your drawing.

Look at the underlined parts of the poem to identify any metaphors that you drew. Remember that a metaphor shows characteristics of one thing by using words associated with something else.

✳ Explain the differences between the lines "Skiing is like being part of a mountain" at the beginning of the poem and "I am the mountain and the mountain is me" at the end of the poem. Discuss your answers with a partner.

_____

_____

_____

_____

✳ You probably recognized the last lines as metaphors. You may see the first line as a metaphor, too, which it is. A metaphor that uses the word *like* in the comparison is a special kind of metaphor called a **simile.** Think of your experiences skiing or watching skiing on television. What similes can you think of to describe a skier?

_____

_____

_____

_____

PERFORMING A POEM

Reread "Skiing." Get into the same group you were in when you performed "Karate Kid" in Lesson 21. Review the guidelines that tell you how to perform a poem. (See page 73.)

✳ For this advanced performance, add four more items to the list:

■ Show confidence when you're in front of the class.

■ Wait for the audience's attention before you begin.

■ Stay near each other when reading or acting.

■ After the applause, take a bow.

Practice your performance of "Skiing," then dramatize it for the class. After all the groups have performed, talk about how your second performance was either better than or not as good as your first.

The power of poetry comes from how well the poet uses figurative language, such as similes and metaphors.

When you read, do you see pictures of what you're reading about? This is a strategy that good readers use. It is called **visualizing.** We learn about things by making pictures in our minds, which we call **images.** The use of this in poetry is called **imagery.**

Read "The Swimmer" by Constance Levy. Notice the images you make as you read. Put check marks next to lines that help you "see" the swimmer and the setting of the poem.

The Swimmer by Constance Levy

The sun
underwater
makes chains of gold
that rearrange
as I reach through.
I feel at home
within this world
of sunlit water, cool and blue.
I sip the air;
I stroke;
I kick;
big bubbles bloom as I breathe out.
Although I have no tail or fin
I'm closer than I've ever been
to what fish feel
and think about. ❖

✳ Reread the lines that you marked. In the **Response Notes** column, draw pictures of the images that these lines of poetry help you see. When you finish, choose two or three of the images you drew. Explain how the poet's language helps you *see* the swimmer.

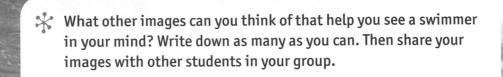

✻ What other images can you think of that help you see a swimmer in your mind? Write down as many as you can. Then share your images with other students in your group.

_____

_____

_____

_____

_____

✻ Use the images you thought of in a short poem of your own.

_____

_____

_____

_____

_____

_____

_____

_____

_____

_____

_____

_____

_____

_____

_____

_____

The poet's choice of words and phrases helps the reader visualize the poem, which helps develop understanding.

Choosing just the right words for a poem is an important part of a poet's work. You've seen how poets use words in metaphors and similes. Sometimes **word choice** is very important, such as in the poem by Robert Francis about a base stealer during a game of baseball.

As you read the poem, notice the words that the poet uses to tell how the base stealer moves. Underline them.

The Base Stealer by Robert Francis

Poised between going on and back, pulled
Both ways taut like a tightrope-walker,
Fingertips pointing the opposites,
Now bouncing tiptoe like a dropped ball
Or a kid skipping rope, come on, come on,
Running a scattering of steps sidewise,
How he teeters, skitters, tingles, teases,
Taunts them, hovers like an ecstatic bird,
He's only flirting, crowd him, crowd him,
Delicate, delicate, delicate, delicate—now! ❖

Response Notes

✳ Look at the words you underlined. Write about these words. Which part of speech are most of the words? How do they show a base stealer at work? Do they speed up the poem or slow it down?

_____

_____

_____

_____

_____

_____

_____

_____

_____

✳ You probably have noticed that the poet used a lot of verbs, or action words, in the poem. Below are some of the verbs from "The Base Stealer." Make notes about as many of them as you can, either drawing the actions or describing them in other words:

teeters

tingles

taunts

teases

skitters

hovers

_____

_____

_____

_____

_____

Did you notice that this poem is all one sentence? It is not a conventional or traditional sentence, but it works like one sentence. When a poet bends the rules a bit, it is called **poetic license.**

✳ Try writing a poem about an athlete setting a record. Use verbs that are vivid and specific. You may wish to use a thesaurus to help you find dramatic word choices. If you want, try to write the poem in one sentence, as Robert Francis has done.

_____

_____

_____

_____

_____

_____

_____

_____

_____

_____

Poets use vivid and specific verbs to help readers see and feel the action of a poem.

In "Foul Shot," poet Edwin A. Hoey used many verbs, as Robert Francis did in "The Base Stealer." Hoey also used language that appeals to your senses, which is **sensory language**.

As you read the poem, mark where the poem uses sensory language. Underline those words and phrases.

Foul Shot by Edwin A. Hoey

With two 60's stuck on the scoreboard
And two seconds hanging on the clock,
The solemn boy in the center of eyes,
Squeezed by silence,
Seeks out the line with his feet,
Soothes his hands along his uniform,
Gently drums the ball against the floor
Then measures the waiting net,
Raises the ball on his right hand,
Balances it with his left,
Calms it with fingertips,
Breathes,
Crouches,
Waits,
And then through a stretching of stillness,
Nudges it upward.

The ball
Slides up and out,
Lands,
Leans,
Wobbles,
Wavers,
Hesitates,
Exasperates,
Plays it coy
Until every face begs with unsounding screams—.

And then
   And then
      And then,
Right before ROAR-UP,
Dives down and through. ✛

Response Notes

✳ Read the poem again. This time, underline all of the action words, or verbs, in the poem. Verbs help the reader "see" the action.

Verbs	How they appeal to the senses

✳ Put an asterisk beside the verbs that you think are most effective in helping you "see" the poem. Choose one of the verbs. Explain why you think it is effective.

WRITE A POEM

✳ Working alone or with a group, list as many names of sports as you can. Use a large sheet of paper, leaving a lot of space between names of sports. Consider including sports other than the usual team sports, like cross-country, skating, dancing, or cheerleading. For each sport listed, create a web of words associated with that sport. Remember to use verbs and images. Use a different color for each sport.

From the big list, choose one sport with which you have experience to serve as the subject of a sports poem you will write. Copy the web for your sport in this space.

✳ Expand the word web with your own experiences in that sport. Use a second color for these words and phrases. Here you can be specific, making notes about "a time when I . . ."

❋ Next, follow the guidelines listed below for writing your sports poem. Consider writing your draft on a separate sheet of paper and then copying the final poem into your *Daybook*.

■ Create a beginning, a middle, and an end for your poem.

■ Use colorful adjectives and vivid verbs.

■ Include important details and create interesting images.

■ Use at least a couple of similes or metaphors. You might also consider using rhyme, rhythm, and line design.

Sensory language is a technique that poets use to make their poems effective and memorable.

Studying an Author

It was simply what I always wanted to do, from childhood: what I did best, loved best. I have never wanted to do anything but write. To shape, to create and compose, to shed light, to perceive and pass on. —Lois Lowry

Where do writers get their ideas? Most writers will tell you that it's a good idea to "write what you know," that the subjects for writing come from life experiences. In many of Lois Lowry's novels, you get glimpses of people in Lowry's family, flashes of places where she has lived, and memories of events she has experienced. But Lowry also charts new worlds that grow out of her imagination.

In this unit, you'll take a close look at Lois Lowry's writing, which includes more than twenty novels, two of them Newbery Medal winners. You'll think about where she gets ideas, as well as the types of issues she explores in her stories. By studying an accomplished author, you will learn how to communicate your thoughts as stories. Your stories will reflect who you are and what you know and imagine.

So often we remember childhood as a continuous bright street of cheerful pleasure, the bright street where we roller-skated over a geography of sidewalks memorized by our feet. The softball games at sunset, the smell of fresh-baked oatmeal cookies, the soft voices of mothers, the stern-but-just wisdom of fathers, and endless summer days – the nights flickering with fireflies – and the clean sheets at bedtime. We forget the dark paths that all children must travel as well.
—from Lois Lowry's speech, *Bright Streets and Dark Paths,* Brown University, March 2001

Life experiences shape our thoughts about the world. Lowry draws on her experiences and the relationships within her family for her stories. In her first novel, *A Summer to Die*, Lowry centers the story on the death of a sister. Thirteen-year-old Meg realizes that her older sister Molly is dying of cancer. Lowry had a similar experience when her sister Helen died of cancer.

In the following excerpt, Meg and her father have a conversation about what is happening to Molly. As you read the dialogue, underline passages that you think are powerful. Reflect on their meaning in your **Response Notes.**

from **A Summer to Die** by Lois Lowry

Response Notes

Dad drove me to Portland, and on the way he tried to tell me what it would be like at the hospital. "You have to keep reminding yourself," he said, "that it's still Molly. That's the hard thing, for me. Every time I go in her room, it takes me by surprise, seeing all that machinery. It seems to separate you from her. You have to look past it, and see that it's still Molly. Do you understand?"

I shook my head. "No," I said.

Dad sighed. "Well, I'm not sure I do either. But listen, Meg—when you think of Molly, how do you think of her?"

I was quiet for a minute, thinking. "I guess mostly I think of how she used to laugh. And then I think of how, even after she got sick, she used to run out in the field on sunny mornings, looking for new flowers. I used to watch her, sometimes, from the window."

"That's what I mean. That's the way I think of Molly, too. But when you get to the hospital, you'll see that everything is different for Molly now. It will make you feel strange, because you're outside of it; you're not part of it.

© GREAT SOURCE. COPYING IS PROHIBITED.

"She'll be very sleepy. That's because of the drugs they're giving her, so that she'll feel comfortable. And she can't talk to you, because there's a tube in her throat to help her breathe.

"She'll look like a stranger to you, at first. And it'll be scary. But she can hear you, Meg. Talk to her. And you'll realize that underneath all that stuff, the tubes and needles and medicines, our Molly is still there. You have to remember that. It makes it easier.

"And, Meg?" He was driving very carefully, following the white line in the center of the curving road.

"What?"

"One more thing. Remember, too, that Molly's not in any pain, and she's not scared. It's only you and I and Mom, now, who are hurting and frightened.

"This is a hard thing to explain, Meg, but Molly is handling this thing very well by herself. She needs us, for our love, but she doesn't need us for anything else now." He swallowed hard and said, "Dying is a very solitary thing. The only thing we can do is be there when she wants us there." ❖

✳ Describe what strikes you as the most powerful moment in the exchange between Meg and her Dad. Explain what you learned in that moment about the experience Meg, Molly, and their mom and dad were going through.

_____

_____

_____

✳ Explain how the moment you described makes you feel.

_____

_____

_____

✳ What details in the passage convey the message that Meg's father is trying to express?

_____

_____

_____

✳️ Like Lowry, you can write about experiences that were powerful moments and ones that helped you learn more about life and
relationships. In the Memory Catalog below, list three important
conversations in your life. They don't need to be sad or serious.

MEMORY CATALOG

Important conversations	Notes on what is important in each and why

✳️ Write a scene that portrays one of the conversations in your
Memory Catalog. Remember, when you write dialogue, you use
quotation marks to show your reader that someone is speaking.

_____

_____

_____

_____

_____

_____

_____

_____

_____

_____

_____

_____

Writers draw on
personal experiences and
relationships to bring to life
powerful moments.

Few things give me more pleasure than looking at photographs. To glimpse other lives, caught and captured in moments that live on long after the circumstances of the moment have passed, makes me shiver with imagination. —Lois Lowry from "Acknowledgments" in *The Silent Boy*

Lois Lowry compares the craft of a writer to a photographer's eye: both must learn to capture details, knowing which things to focus on and which to blur. One of Lowry's novels, *The Silent Boy*, was inspired by a collection of photographs. These photographs—taken of family and others and found in an antique shop—inspired her characters and the events of the novel. A photo introduces the events of each chapter. In the following scene, the narrator, Katy, sees a photograph that reminds her of a summer day when she was four.

As you read the excerpt from *The Silent Boy,* try to imagine the setting. Think about what pictures come to your mind as you read. Underline words and phrases that help you see, hear, touch, taste, and smell the scene. Make notes about the connections you make to your life.

from **The Silent Boy** by Lois Lowry

Response Notes

I peered at the photograph of two solemn little girls, side by side, wearing hats, and gradually I remembered that day at the lake. It was summer. It came to me in fragments, in little details.

Jessie had black shoes, and mine were white.

The air smelled like pine trees.

A cloud was shaped like my stuffed bear. Then its ears softened and smeared, and it was just a cloud, really, not a bear at all (I knew it all along); then, quickly, the cloud itself was gone and the sky was only blue.

And there were fireworks! We were visiting at the Woods' cottage there. Cottage sounded like a fairy tale: a woodcutter's cottage. Hansel and Gretel and their cottage.

But the Woods' cottage was not a fairy-tale storybook one. It was just a house. They invited my family to come to their cottage for the holiday called Fourthofjuly, which I didn't understand, and for fireworks.

I remembered the scent, the sky, the heat, the wide-brimmed straw hats we wore to protect our faces from the sun, and the white shoes and black. The shoes and stockings and dresses—even the hats—were removed, at some point, because my memory told of Jessie and me, wearing only our bloomers,

wading at the edge of the lake. We chased tiny silvery fish—minnows! Someone told us they were called minnows, and we said that to each other, laughing: "Minnows! Minnows!"

After a while we were shivering, even though the day was hot. My fingertips were puckered, pale lavender. Our mothers rubbed us dry with rough
towels. Jessie fretted because there were pine needles stuck to her damp feet.
We played in the sand at the edge of the lake.

The parents sat on the porch, talking, while Jessie and I amused ourselves,
still half-naked in the sunshine, digging with bent tin shovels in the damp
sand. Jessie had a pail and I didn't. I pretended that I didn't care about her
pail, though secretly I wished it were mine, with the bright painted picture
printed on its metal side: pink-faced children building castles, green-blue
water, foamed with white, curling behind them.

Stealthily I followed a beige toad that hopped heavily away into the grasses
edging the small beach. Soon I could no longer see the toad (I had begun to
think of him as "my" toad) but when I waited, silent, I saw the grass move
and knew that he had hopped again. I waited, watched. I followed where the
grass moved. It was taller than my head, now, and I was surrounded by it and
was briefly frightened, feeling that I had become invisible and not-there with
the high reeds around me. But the world continued close by. I could hear the
grownups talking on the porch, still.

"Where's Katy?" I heard my mother ask, suddenly.

"Jessie where did Katy go?" Mrs. Wood called in an unconcerned voice.

"I don't know." Jessie's voice was not that far away from me.

"She was right there. I saw her just a minute ago." That was my
father's voice.

"It's amazing, how quickly they scamper off, isn't it?" Mrs. Wood again.
She was using a cheerful voice, but I could tell that now she was worried, and
I was made pleased and proud by the worry.

"Katy!" My mother was calling now. "Katy!"

I should call back, I knew. But I liked the feeling of being concealed there,
squatting in the moist earth, with the high grass golden above me, being an

observer, but hidden. The breeze blew the grass and it closed above my head, creating a small, secret place where I fit. I had already forgotten my toad in the new excitement of being lost to the grownups. So I held still.

"You go that way, Caroline," my father said. "Check over there behind the woodpile and by the shed. I'll look in this direction."

"She wouldn't have gone into the house, would she? She would have had to pass us, to go into the house. We would have seen her. Katy!"

"Jessie, are you sure you don't know where she went?" Mr. Wood sounded angry, as if he were scolding his little girl.

Jessie began to cry. It pleased me somehow, that she was crying. She deserved to cry, because she owned a tin pail with bright paintings on its side.

"Katy! Katy!" My mother's voice was quite far from me now.

"Let's think." Jessie's mother said this. "*Hush*, Jessie." (Jessie was still crying loudly.) "She wouldn't have gone far because she was barefoot. It's stony out there beyond the house. It would hurt her feet."

"Kaaaaty!" It was like a song in my mother's voice, when she called it that way. "Henry," she called to my father, "she isn't over this way."

"Everyone be absolutely quiet for a moment," Mr. Wood commanded. "She might be calling and we wouldn't hear her."

It was silent except for Jessie, who was now howling. In my mind, I scolded Jessie for not obeying her father. "Shhhh," Mrs. Wood said to her angrily, and finally Jessie was quiet.

Now, into that important silence, was when I should have called out. "Surprise!" I should have shouted. "Here I am!"

But I didn't. I waited. There was a bug near my toe, and I watched it waddle across the slick surface of wet earth. I put my hand near it and hoped that it would mount my finger and walk on me. But carefully it found a path around my hand. I began thinking very hard about the bug, and I forgot my family and their worry. I crouched there, and then lay down, slowly curling into the warm mud that was as soft and private as a bed. The sun was hot on my head and back, coming down through the curtain of grass that surrounded me, and things became dreamlike. ❖

✳ A storyboard helps you keep track of different scenes in passages that you are reading. Use the frames on the next page to sketch three "snapshots" from the scene you just read. Under each sketch write a quote from the text that shows where the idea came from. When you finish, share your sketches and quotes with a partner.

Storyboard for Scenes

1	2	3

✳ Lowry worked from a photograph to imagine the scene you read. Now, it's your turn. Use this scene in the photograph to tell a story. Remember to use visual and sensory details in the way that Lowry used them in her scene.

_____

_____

_____

_____

_____

_____

_____

_____

_____

_____

_____

_____

Writers use the world around them to get ideas for stories in which they explore people, situations, and issues.

The Giver begins with a boy on a bicycle, riding through the clean and safe streets of his community to the dwelling where he lives with his happy, cheerful, busy family. It concludes with the same boy riding a bicycle at night—hiding by day—for many miles, through terrible danger. He saves himself—quite literally saves himself; warms and nourishes himself and finds courage—by recalling the stories from the past that have been told to him by an old man.—from Lois Lowry's speech, *Bright Streets and Dark Paths,* Brown University, March 2001

What kind of world could Lowry have imagined that would change the boy's life so dramatically? *The Giver* is set in the future. Lowry creates a world of *sameness* where the climate is controlled and the inhabitants' lives are monitored. Each family has two parents, a daughter, and a son, but they are not biologically related; they are developed through careful observation and placement.

As you read the following excerpt, use your **Response Notes** to ask questions about the type of world in which the characters live. List issues that you think Lowry examines in her imagined world.

from **The Giver** by Lois Lowry

Response Notes

"I heard about a guy who was absolutely certain he was going to be assigned Engineer," Asher muttered as they ate, "and instead they gave him Sanitation Laborer. He went out the next day, jumped into the river, swam across, and joined the next community he came to. Nobody ever saw him again."

Jonas laughed. "Somebody made that story up, Ash," he said. "My father said he heard that story when *he* was a Twelve."

But Asher wasn't reassured. He was eyeing the river where it was visible behind the Auditorium. "I can't even swim very well," he said. "My swimming instructor said that I don't have the right boyishness or something."

"Buoyancy," Jonas corrected him.

"Whatever. I don't have it. I sink."

"Anyway," Jonas pointed out, "have you ever once known of anyone—I mean really known for sure, Asher, not just heard a story about it—who joined another community?"

"No," Asher admitted reluctantly. "But you can. It says so in the rules. If you don't fit in, you can apply for Elsewhere and be released. My mother says that once, about ten years ago, someone applied and was gone the next day." Then he chuckled. "She told me that because I was driving her crazy. She threatened to apply for Elsewhere."

"She was joking."

"I know. But it was true, what she said, that someone did that once. She said that it was really true. Here today and gone tomorrow. Never seen again. Not even a Ceremony of Release."

Jonas shrugged. It didn't worry him. How could someone not fit in? The community was so meticulously ordered, the choices so carefully made.

Even the Matching of Spouses was given such weighty consideration that sometimes an adult who applied to receive a spouse waited months or even *years* before a Match was approved and announced. All of the factors—disposition, energy level, intelligence, and interests—had to correspond and to interact perfectly. Jonas's mother, for example, had higher intelligence than his father; but his father had a calmer disposition. They balanced each other. Their Match, which like all Matches had been monitored by the Committee of Elders for three years before they could apply for children, had always been a successful one.

Like the Matching of Spouses and the Naming and Placement of new children, the Assignments were scrupulously thought through by the Committee of Elders.

He was certain that his Assignment, whatever it was to be, and Asher's too, would be the right one for them. He only wished that the midday break would conclude, that the audience would reenter the Auditorium, and the suspense would end.

As if in answer to his unspoken wish, the signal came and the crowd began to move toward the doors. ❖

❋ Write a paragraph describing your reactions and feelings about the type of society in which Asher and Jonas are living. What type of society is this? What do the rules seem to be?

_____

_____

_____

_____

_____

_____

_____

✳ What issues in society does Lowry seem to be exploring through this imagined world? Use the following chart to help you look back at the text and draw conclusions from information in the text.

DRAWING CONCLUSIONS

Quotes from the text	What I conclude

✳ If you could design a future world, what would it be like? Take a minute to brainstorm the characteristics of your society, using the Future-World Chart to prompt your thinking.

FUTURE-WORLD CHART

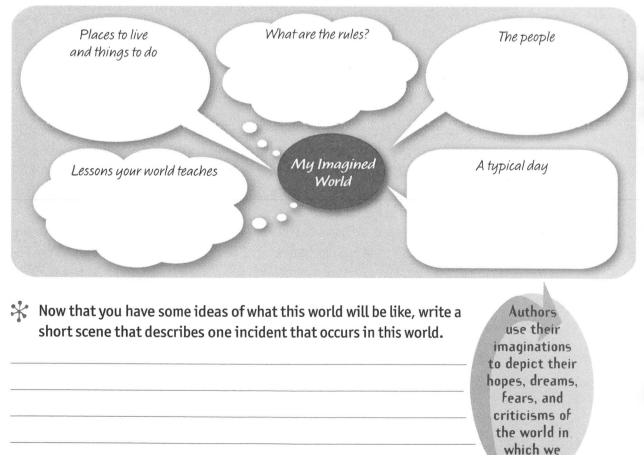

Places to live and things to do

What are the rules?

The people

Lessons your world teaches

My Imagined World

A typical day

✳ Now that you have some ideas of what this world will be like, write a short scene that describes one incident that occurs in this world.

Authors use their imaginations to depict their hopes, dreams, fears, and criticisms of the world in which we live.

_____
_____
_____
_____
_____

EXPLORING IDEAS THROUGH FICTION

There is always a period of time, after I have written a book, before it is published, when I begin to worry that my brain has simply run out and become empty, the way a cookie jar does, and all the good stuff is gone; only a stiff raisin and some stale crumbs left. I worry then that I will never be able to write the next one. —from Lois Lowry's speech, *How Everything Turns Away,* University of Richmond, March 2005.

Lowry doesn't seem to come up short on ideas, although she worries that she will. Not long after *The Giver* was published, she completed a companion novel, *Gathering Blue*. In it, Lowry explores a different *"what if"* proposition than she did in *The Giver*. *What if* a society hasn't moved forward technologically as in *The Giver* where everything is controlled and engineered? *What if* the society has become primitive and savage? *What if,* instead of controlling everything, even memory, organized society has collapsed?

As you read the following excerpt from *Gathering Blue,* underline words or phrases that demonstrate the decline of this society compared to the society in *The Giver*.

Response Notes

from Gathering Blue by Lois Lowry

With the boy still beside her, Kira paused at the well and filled her container with water. Everywhere she heard arguing. The cadence of bickering was a constant sound in the village: the harsh remarks of men vying for power; the shrill bragging and taunting of women envious of one another and irritable with the tykes who whined and whimpered at their feet and were frequently kicked out of the way.

She cupped her hand over her eyes and squinted against the afternoon sun to find the gap where her own cott had been. She took a deep breath. It would be a long walk to gather saplings and a hard chore to dig the mud by the riverbank. The corner timbers would be heavy to lift and hard to drag. "I have to start building," she told Matt, who still held a bundle of twigs in his scratched, dirty arms. "Do you want to help? It could be fun if there were two of us.

"I can't pay you, but I'll tell you some new stories," she added.

The boy shook his head. "I be whipped iffen I don't finish the fire twiggies." He turned away. After a hesitation, he turned back to Kira and said in a low voice, "I heared them talking. They don't want you should stay. They be planning to turn you out, now your mum be dead. They be putting you in the Field for the beasts. They talk about having draggers take you."

Kira felt her stomach tighten with fear. But she tried to keep her voice calm. She needed information from Matt and it would make him wary to know she was frightened. "Who's 'they'?" she asked in an annoyed, superior tone.

"Them women," he replied. "I heard them talking at the well. I be picking up wood chippies from the refuse, and them didn't even notice me listening. But they want your space. They want where your cott was. They aim to build a pen there, to keep the tykes and the fowls enclosed so they don't be having to chase them all the time."

Kira stared at him. It was terrifying, almost unbelievable, the casualness of their cruelty. In order to pen their disobedient toddlers and chickens, the women would turn her out of the village to be devoured by the beasts that waited in the woods to forage the Field. ✛

✳ Write a paragraph describing your reactions and feelings about the type of society in which Kira and Matt are living. What type of society is this? What do the rules seem to be?

_____

_____

_____

_____

_____

_____

✳ Be the author and write the next scene in *Gathering Blue.*

_____

_____

_____

_____

_____

_____

_____

_____

✳ Now that you have read excerpts from *The Giver* and *Gathering Blue*, list the characteristics of each society.

■ Compare characters' concerns and fears.

■ Compare what life is like.

■ Compare the relationships within families.

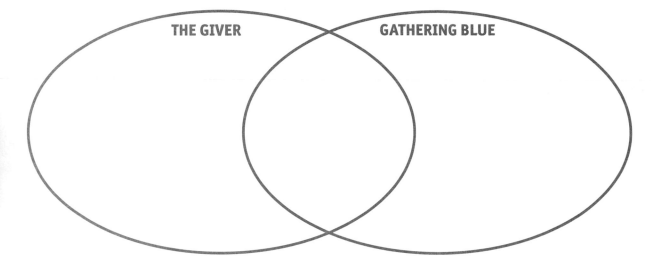

THE GIVER   **GATHERING BLUE**

✳ Write a paragraph that compares and contrasts the two worlds that Lowry imagines. What aspect of these two cultures is most disturbing to you? Tell why.

_____

_____

_____

_____

_____

_____

_____

_____

_____

_____

_____

Writers use their writing to explore *what if* certain things happened in the world.

"I practiced in my spiral-bound notebooks: making sentences, rearranging them to say the same thing in a different ordering of words, then saying it again in new words so that I could compare the sound, and the way the words looked on the page." —from Lois Lowry's speech *The Remembered Gate and the Unopened Door*, Chicago Public Library, May 4, 2001.

Writing was what Lois Lowry always wanted to do. She began to write in elementary school. In the excerpt below, Lowry tells the story of her first typewriter and its importance to her work as a writer.

In your **Response Notes,** note what Lowry reveals about the importance of writing and her purposes for writing.

from "The Remembered Gate and the Unopened Door"
The Sutherland Lecture, May 4, 2001

Response Notes

On my thirteenth birthday, my father gave me a typewriter. Today, of course, half the 13-year-olds you know have their own computers. But this was in 1950. And in 1950 this was an astounding gift: a Smith-Corona portable typewriter with smooth dark green keys; and my name was engraved on the case, just below the handle.

Why did he give it to me? I don't know. It may have been simply that he was sick of my sneaking into his office and using <u>his</u> typewriter; maybe he was nervous about the damage I might inflict as I endlessly, noisily taught myself how to type.

But I like to think that he gave it to me because he recognized who I was, and what my dreams were, for the future. And I am immeasurably grateful that he never—never once—leaned over my shoulder, to see what I was doing with my gift.

I used that typewriter through high school and college. It went into a closet, along with my dreams of being a writer, and stayed there, unused, through an early marriage and the arrival of four children. But it came out of storage and was dusted off when I went to graduate school and began to write, in my thirties. I used the old Smith-Corona to write my first book for kids, *A Summer to Die.* I was thirty-nine.

My father was over seventy by then: retired, living in Florida. He sent me a gift to celebrate the publication of that first book, in which he appeared, as Meg's father. It was an electric typewriter.

Response Notes

I began—after a protracted education, after interruptions, (sometimes happy ones like the births of babies), and after a few false starts, as a writer for adults. . . . But it was not until I went back and timidly pulled at unopened doors in my past that I realized I should be speaking to children.

I am not certain how I knew I must do that. But it was as if, as a writer, I was still in a passageway, or a vestibule, and had not reached the place I needed to go. ❖

※ You've been chosen to write about the author for the cover of Lois Lowry's new book. In your critical acclaim, use what you have learned—about Lowry as a person and as a writer—to describe the author and her writing.

_____

_____

_____

_____

_____

_____

※ What can you use as a lesson from Lowry in your future writing? What have you learned about yourself as a writer through the writing you have done in this unit? Think about the ways in which you work, what you like to write about, and what sources you draw on for ideas.

_____

_____

_____

_____

_____

_____

Writers use many different sources of information and inspiration to express the purposes and subjects of their writing.

Assessing Your Growing Repertoire

When you reach this point in the *Daybook*, you have been introduced to a number of ways to become a better reader and writer. You have learned how to interact and connect with the stories and articles you are reading. You have used multiple perspectives. You have looked carefully at language and craft. You have spent time focused on one particular author. Now we are going to put all of those skills and strategies into one unit, ending with an opportunity for you to write a story that shows how well you can organize and express your ideas.

You are going to read two Native American teaching stories, "Eagle Boy" and "Salmon Boy," as told by Joseph Bruchac. You will participate in a number of reading and writing activities designed to show how well you use the skills and strategies presented. You will work both individually and in groups as you read, talk, draw, and write.

After you have written and revised your final assessment paper, you will make judgments about your ability to apply the skills and strategies you have learned. And you will think about what you need to do to further improve your reading and writing as you continue to build your repertoire of essential skills.

USING READING AND WRITING STRATEGIES

In the previous units, you practiced using reading strategies such as making connections to the text and examining the author's perspective. Each lesson focused on one strategy or idea. A successful reader, however, knows which strategy to choose and often uses more than one per selection.

BEFORE YOU READ

You should know that this story is one that Native American parents, aunts, and uncles use to teach their values to their children. Most native people of North America think of animals as beings equal to humans. Stories of animals becoming people and people becoming animals are common. They believe that animals have their own families and traditions and that human beings can learn how to live in harmony with the earth by understanding the animal world.

DURING YOUR READING

Use the Response Notes column to record your ideas and feelings as you read "Eagle Boy." Remember, you can make predictions, write questions, notice what surprises you, and make connections to what you already know.

"Eagle Boy" by Joseph Bruchac

Response Notes

Long ago, a boy was out walking one day when he found a young eagle had fallen from its nest. He picked that eagle up and brought it home and began to care for it. He made a place for it to stay, and each day he went out and hunted for rabbits and other small game to feed it. His mother asked him why he no longer came to work in the fields and help his family. "I must hunt for this eagle," the boy said. So it went on for a long time and the eagle grew large and strong as the boy hunted and fed it. Now it was large enough to fly away if it wished, but it stayed with the boy who had cared for it so well. The boy's brothers criticized him for not doing his part to care for the corn fields and the melon fields, but Eagle Boy did not hear them. He cared only for his bird. Even the boy's father, who was an important man in the village, began to criticize him for not helping. But still the boy did not listen. So it was that the boy's brothers and his older male relatives came together and decided that they must kill the eagle. They decided they would do so when they returned from the fields on the following day.

When Eagle Boy came to his bird's cage, he saw that the bird sat there with its head down. He placed a rabbit he had just caught in the cage, but the eagle did not touch it.

"What is wrong, my eagle?" said the boy.

Then the eagle spoke, even though it had never spoken before. "My friend, I cannot eat because I am filled with sorrow," said the eagle.

"Why are you troubled?" said the boy.

"It is because of you," said the eagle. "You have not done your work in the fields. Instead, you have spent all of your time caring for me. Now your brothers and your older male relatives have decided to kill me so that you will again return to your duties in the village. I have stayed here all of this time because I love you. But now I must leave. When the sun rises tomorrow, I will fly away and never come back."

"My eagle," said the boy, "I do not wish to stay here without you. You must take me with you."

"My friend, I cannot take you with me," said the eagle. "You would not be able to find your way through the sky. You would not be able to eat raw food."

"My eagle," said the boy, "I cannot live here without you." So he begged the eagle and at last the great bird agreed.

"If you are certain, then you may come with me. But you must do as I say. Come to me at dawn, after the people have gone down to their fields. Bring food to eat on our long journey across the sky. Put the food in pouches that you can sling over your shoulders. You must also bring two strings of bells and tie them to my feet."

That night the boy filled pouches with blue corn wafer bread and dried meat and fruits. He made up two strings of bells, tying them with strong rawhide. The next morning, after the people had gone down to the fields, he went to the eagle's cage and opened it. The eagle spread its wings wide.

"Now," he said to Eagle Boy, "'tie the bells to my feet and then climb onto my back and hold onto the base of my wings."

Eagle Boy climbed on and the eagle began to fly. It rose higher and higher in slow circles above the town and above the field. The bells on the eagle's feet jingled and the eagle sang and the boy sang with it:

> Huli-i-i, hu-li-i-i
> Pa shish lakwa-a-a-a . . .

So they sang and the people in the fields below heard them singing, and they heard the sounds of the bells Eagle Boy had tied to the eagle's feet. They all looked up.

"They are leaving," the people said. "They are leaving." Eagle Boy's parents called up to him to return, but he could not hear them. The eagle and the boy rose higher and higher in the sky until they were only a tiny speck and then they were gone from the sight of the village people.

The eagle and the boy flew higher and higher until they came to an opening in the clouds. They passed through and came out into the Sky Land. They landed there on Turquoise Mountain where the Eagle People lived. Eagle Boy looked around the sky world. Everything was smooth and white and clean as clouds.

"Here is my home," the eagle said. He took the boy into the city in the sky, and there were eagles all around them. They looked like people, for they took off their wings and their clothing of feathers when they were in their homes.

The Eagle People made a coat of eagle feathers for the boy and taught him to wear it and to fly. It took him a long time to learn, but soon he was able to circle above the land just like the Eagle People and he was an eagle himself.

"You may fly anywhere," the old eagles told him, "anywhere except to the south. Never fly to the South Land."

All went well for Eagle Boy in his new life. One day, though, as he flew alone, he wondered what it was that was so terrible about the south. His curiosity grew, and he flew further and further toward the south. Lower and lower he flew and now he saw a beautiful city below with people dancing around red fires.

"There is nothing to fear here," he said, and flew lower still. Closer and closer he came, drawn by the red fires, until he landed The people greeted him and drew him into the circle. He danced with them all night and then, when he grew tired, they gave him a place to sleep. When he woke next morning and looked around, he saw that the fires were gone. The houses no longer seemed bright and beautiful. All around him there was dust, and in the dust there were bones. He looked for his cloak of eagle feathers, wanting to fly away from this city of the dead, but it was nowhere to be found. Then the bones rose up and came together. There were people made of bones all around him! He rose and began to run, and the people made of bones chased him. Just as they were about to catch him, he saw a badger.

"Grandson," the badger said, "I will save you." Then the badger carried the boy down into his hole and the bone people could not follow. "You have been foolish," the badger said. "You did not listen to the warnings the eagles gave you. Now that you have been to this land in the south, they will not allow you to live with them anymore."

Then the badger showed Eagle Boy the way back to the city of the eagles. It was a long journey and when the boy reached the eagle city, he stood outside the high white walls. The eagles would not let him enter.

"You have been to the South Land," they said. "'You can no longer live with us."

At last the eagle the boy had raised took pity on him. He brought the boy an old and ragged feather cloak.

"With this cloak you may reach the home of your own people," he said. "But you can never return to our place in the sky."

So the boy took the cloak of tattered feathers. His flight back down to his people was a hard one and he almost fell many times. When he landed on the earth in his village, the eagles flew down and carried off his feathered cloak. From then on, Eagle Boy lived among his people. Though he lifted his eyes and watched whenever eagles soared overhead, he shared in the work in the fields, and his people were glad to have him among them. ❖

AFTER YOU READ

❋ Look at your **Response Notes.** Write a few lines about what this story made you think about and how this story made you feel.

✳ Get together with your group and talk about the story "Eagle Boy." Below are three questions that might help you as you think and talk about the story. After you have talked with your group, write the group's ideas and your ideas that address these questions.

1 What did you find hard to understand about the story?

2 Why did Eagle Boy go to the South Land?

3 What did Eagle Boy learn from his experience?

What the Group Thought	What I Think Now
1 What the group found hard to understand	1 What I find hard to understand
2 Why the group thought Eagle Boy went to South Land	2 Why I think Eagle Boy went to South Land
3 What the group thought Eagle Boy learned	3 What I think Eagle Boy learned

✳ What did you learn by discussing the three questions with your group? What ideas did you contribute to the group? Did any of you change your minds or understand the story better as the result of what other members said? Write a few sentences that tell what was important about your group discussion.

_____

_____

_____

_____

_____

_____

What do you think children who were told this story were supposed to learn?

_____

_____

_____

_____

_____

_____

Effective readers sometimes use more than one strategy when they read a piece of writing.

BEFORE YOU READ

You should know that the story about Eagle Boy is told by the Zuni people who live in the southwestern part of the United States. The next story you will read is from the Haida nation, which is in the Pacific Northwest. The Haida people depend on salmon for their livelihoods. It is very important to the Haida people that everyone in the community respects the salmon.

DURING YOUR READING

Use the **Response Notes** to record your ideas and feelings as you read. You can make predictions, sketch what you visualize, or write connections that you make.

"Salmon Boy" by Joseph Bruchac

Response Notes

Long ago, among the Haida people, there was a boy who showed no respect for the salmon. Though the salmon meant life for the people, he was not respectful of the one his people called Swimmer. His parents told him to show gratitude and behave properly, but he did not listen. When fishing he would step on the bodies of the salmon that were caught and after eating he carelessly threw the bones of the fish into the bushes. Others warned him that the spirits of the salmon were not pleased by such behavior, but he did not listen.

One day, his mother served him a meal of salmon. He looked at it with disgust. "This is moldy," he said, though the meat was good. He threw it upon the ground. Then he went down to the river to swim with the other children. However, as he was swimming, a current caught him and pulled him away from the others. It swept him into the deepest water and he could not swim strongly enough to escape from it. He sank into the river and drowned.

There, deep in the river, the Salmon People took him with them. They were returning back to the ocean without their bodies. They had left their bodies behind for the humans and the animal people to use as food. The boy went with them, for he now belonged to the salmon.

When they reached their home in the ocean, they looked just like human beings. Their village there in the ocean looked much like his own home and he could hear the sound of children playing in the stream which flowed behind the village. Now the Salmon People began to teach him. He was hungry and they told him to go to the stream and catch one of their children, who were salmon swimming in the stream. However, he was told, he must be respectful and after eating return all of the bones and everything he did not intend to eat to the water. Then, he was told, their child would be able to come back to life. But if the bones were not returned to the water, that salmon child could not come back.

He did as he was told, but one day after he had eaten, when it came time for the children to come up to the village from the stream he heard one of them crying. He went to see what was wrong. The child was limping because one of its feet was gone. Then the boy realized he had not thrown all of the fins back into the stream. He quickly found the one fin he had missed, threw it in and the child was healed.

After he had spent the winter with the Salmon People, it again was spring and time for them to return to the rivers. The boy swam with them, for he belonged to the Salmon People now. When they swam past his village, his own mother caught him in her net. When she pulled him from the water, even though he was in the shape of a salmon, she saw the copper necklace he was wearing. It was the same necklace she had given her son. She carried Salmon Boy carefully back home. She spoke to him and held him and gradually he began to shed his salmon skin. First his head emerged. Then, after eight days, he shed all of the skin and was a human again.

Salmon Boy taught the people all of the things he had learned. He was a healer now and helped them when they were sick.

"I cannot stay with you long," he said, "you must remember what I teach you."

He remained with the people until the time came when the old salmon who had gone upstream and not been caught by the humans or the animal people came drifting back down toward the sea. As Salmon Boy stood by the water, he saw a huge old salmon floating down toward him. It was so worn by its journey that he could see through its sides. He recognized it as his own soul and he thrust his spear into it. As soon as he did so, he died.

Then the people of the village did as he had told them to do. They placed his body into the river. It circled four times and then sank, going back to his home in the ocean, back to the Salmon People. ✣

What are your first thoughts and feelings after reading "Salmon Boy"? Review your **Response Notes** for ideas about what to write. Write what this story made you think or wonder about and how it made you feel.

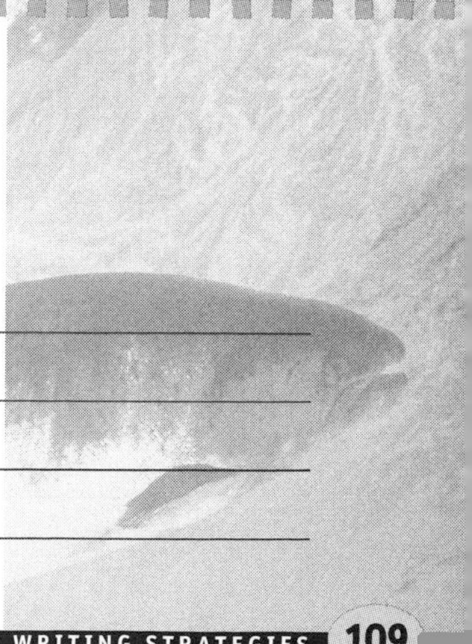

Pick out a part of the story that you thought was important. In the space below, draw what you think this part looked like.

 On the lines below, write why you chose this part of the story.

_____

_____

_____

AFTER READING

 Get together with your group and talk about the story "Salmon Boy." The questions below might help as you think and talk about it. Record your thoughts about each question on the lines.

1 What was hard to understand about this story? _____

_____

_____

2 What did Salmon Boy learn from the salmon?_____

_____

_____

3 Why do you think Salmon Boy thrust his spear into the old salmon at the end of the story?_____

_____

_____

Many teaching stories deal with the survival of the tribe.

CHOOSING A TOPIC FOR WRITING

Remember that the Native peoples used these stories because they believed animals had important lessons to teach human beings. What qualities or values do the eagle and the salmon represent for the Native American people in these stories?

The EAGLE represents ______________________

The SALMON represents ______________________

- Native American parents, aunts and uncles told these stories to help teach children about values and behavior important to their people. In the chart below, write what you think each story was trying to teach.

What Parents Were Trying to Teach in "Eagle Boy"	What Parents Were Trying to Teach in "Salmon Boy"

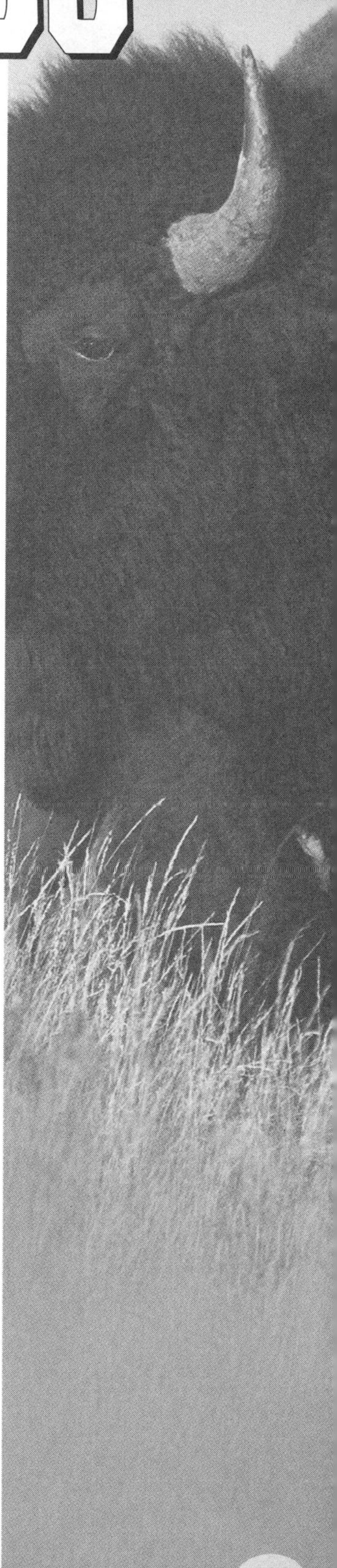

CHOOSING AN ADVENTURE

If you could have one of these two adventures, which would you prefer? Would you rather be Eagle Boy and learn how it is to live among the eagles in Sky Land? Or would you rather learn how to live in a village in the ocean?

- I would rather have the adventures of

____

- Here are my reasons for choosing this adventure:

____

____

____

____

____

Get together with your group and discuss some things that you think are important in your life. These are your values. You might talk about values such as: friendship, honesty, respect. You might talk about how you value the trees and forests. You might talk about how important animals are to the planet.

Discuss things you all value. Then think of animals that are thought to have these qualities. For example, the owl is thought to have wisdom; the lion, strength. The panther is known for speed. The dog is known for faithfulness and the cat for independence.

❋ For your assessment, you are going to write a story of an adventure you have with an animal that has an important quality or value. This value is something you want to learn. First, think about the values that are important to you. Jot some notes here. Discuss these values with your group.

_____

_____

_____

❋ Choose from your list of values one that you want to learn more about. This will be the topic for your assessment story. Write the name of that value here:

_____

❋ Now think of an animal that has the qualities that could teach a lesson about your value. Write the name of your animal here. Explain how that animal represents your value.

_____

_____

_____

_____

Here are some ideas to talk and think about as you prepare to write. Share your ideas with your partner or group. Be sure everyone has a chance to share.

- What value do you want to learn? What animal did you choose to teach it to you?
- What kind of adventure would teach you the lesson you have to learn?
- How does it feel when you change into that animal?
- What happens to you when you are changed into this animal?
    * Where do you go?
    * What do you do?
    * How do you learn your lesson?
    * How do you feel when you are changed back?

Make notes here:

_____

_____

_____

_____

_____

_____

_____

In the box below, draw a picture of your animal teaching you an important lesson.

Thinking about values helps readers focus on key issues.

34 WRITING YOUR ASSESSMENT STORY

You are now ready to write your story for the assessment. Your main character has already been transformed into an animal. On a separate sheet of paper, write about an adventure that the main character has with the teacher animal. The character must learn the lesson taught by the animal. (Remember that the teacher and the learner are now the same type of animal.)

SHARING THE FIRST DRAFT WITH YOUR PARTNER OR GROUP

Meet with your partner or group to share the first draft of your story. Before you read each other's papers, consider these criteria for a successful story.

An outstanding story will

* identify the value that the main character is going to learn.
* explain how the main character meets the animal that is to teach the lesson.
* explain how it feels for the main character to transform into an animal.
* describe the adventure, telling
  - where the main character goes
  - what the main character does
  - how the main character learns his or her lesson
  - how the main character feels when he or she is changed back
* use an interesting selection of words.
* use a variety of sentence types: simple, compound, complex.
* use correct punctuation, capitalization, and spelling.

Read your story aloud to a partner or a small group. Listen carefully to each story. At the end of each story, tell what you liked about it. Use the list in the box above to help give constructive feedback.

As your group talks about your story, make notes so that when you revise it, you will remember what they suggested.

> Setting criteria for writing helps in drafting and revising.

Reread the list of criteria for an outstanding paper on page 114. Using your notes, review your draft carefully to decide how you can improve it.

Now make a clean copy of the final draft of your story. Remember to give it a title that hints at the story.

A FINAL REFLECTION

As you have worked through this half of the book, you have had many opportunities to learn and practice skills and strategies to become a better reader and writer. You have developed and practiced five essential strategies for critical reading and writing:

- Interacting with the text
- Making connections
- Exploring multiple perspectives
- Focusing on language and craft
- Studying an author

You have read a lot of stories, poems, and essays, using such skills and strategies as predicting, questioning, summarizing, visualizing, and reflecting.

In the reflection on page 116, consider how much you have improved as a reader and writer through your work with this first half of the Daybook. Think about the elements and skills that you still need to practice to become a more effective and confident reader and writer.

Write a paragraph reflecting on how you have improved and what you can do to become an even stronger reader and writer.

_____

_____

_____

_____

_____

_____

_____

_____

_____

_____

_____

_____

_____

_____

Reflecting on progress provides guidelines for improvement.

Expanding Your Repertoire

Think of an issue you feel so passionate about that you would take a stand on it. Imagine that you have a week to convince your classmates to feel the same way. What would you do to **persuade** them? To be effective, you would probably try a variety of strategies—not just one. You could also try a variety of genres, or different types of writing: an essay, an article, a song or poem, or even a story. In this unit, you will examine how authors use a variety of genres to persuade readers to think about an important moral issue: having the courage to stand up against indifference and oppression. You will do some persuading of your own, too.

As we discussed in the first unit in this *Daybook*, being a strong reader requires that you build a **repertoire** that helps you become more skilled. Your repertoire is never completely "built." But, the more you expand and use your repertoire, the stronger you'll become.

LESSON 36 · INTERACTING WITH THE TEXT

When you engage with text, you don't simply see the words on the page. You **interact** with them. That means you react, remember, wonder about, ask questions, and get ideas. Also, you allow space for the text to "talk back to you," as if you're having a conversation with it. To do this, you need to listen to what the text has to say. It's important to stop reading sometimes. Give yourself time to think and "listen." Reread sentences or sections if that will help you "converse" with the text. In this lesson, you'll practice not only carrying on your side of the "conversation," but also working hard to "listen" to what the text says to you.

The first excerpt is from a **speech** given at the White House by the author and Nobel Peace Prize winner, Elie Wiesel. One of his most famous books, *Night*, is about his experience surviving in a concentration camp during the Holocaust. In your **Response Notes**, jot down thoughts, questions, or reactions that help you consider what Wiesel **persuades** listeners to think about. Remember, it's okay to pause to think and "listen" as you have a conversation with the text.

from "The Perils of Indifference" by Elie Wiesel

Response Notes

In a way, to be indifferent to that suffering is what makes the human being inhuman. Indifference, after all, is more dangerous than anger and hatred. Anger can at times be creative. One writes a great poem, a great symphony. One does something special for the sake of humanity because one is angry at the injustice that one witnesses. But indifference is never creative. Even hatred at times may elicit a response. You fight it. You denounce it. You disarm it.

Indifference elicits no response. Indifference is not a response. Indifference is not a beginning; it is an end. And, therefore, indifference is always the friend of the enemy, for it benefits the aggressor—never his victim, whose pain is magnified when he or she feels forgotten. The political prisoner in his cell, the hungry children, the homeless refugees—not to respond to their plight, not to relieve their solitude by offering them a spark of hope is to exile them from human memory. And in denying their humanity, we betray our own.

Indifference, then, is not only a sin, it is a punishment. ❖

✳ In every sentence, Wiesel makes us think. Summarize what
you think he is **persuading** us to think about. Is he also
asking us to do something?

_____

_____

_____

_____

_____

_____

✳ Choose one sentence from the excerpt that you responded to in
your notes—one you don't agree with or understand or one that
just makes you think. Record the sentence in the chart below,
then have a "conversation" with it. If it would help to reread
parts of the speech, to look up something in the dictionary,
or to ask another reader a question, do that.

THE SENTENCE	YOUR "CONVERSATION" WITH THE SENTENCE What do you have to say about it? What does it have to say back to you?

Persuasive writing can also take the form of a poem. Read the poem below. In your **Response Notes** jot down questions and reactions as you think about what Hughes is **persuading** you to consider.

"To You" by Langston Hughes

To sit and dream, to sit and read,
To sit and learn about the world
Outside our world of here and now—
    Our problem world—
To dream of vast horizons of the soul
Through dreams made whole,
Unfettered, free—help me!
All you who are dreamers too,
    Help me to make
Our world anew.
I reach out my dreams to you. ❖

✻ Explain what Hughes is persuading us to think about or do.

_____

_____

_____

✻ Choose two or three lines from the poem. Record the lines in the Double-entry Journal below, then have a "conversation" with them.

LINES FROM POEM	YOUR "CONVERSATION" WITH THESE LINES What do you have to say about them? What do these lines have to say back to you?

Interact with the text by making notes, "listening" to what the text says to you, and pausing to think what you have to say back to the text.

As you already know, there are many ways to **make connections** as you read. You can connect the text to you, to other texts, and to other things you know about. It 's important to connect *back* to the text, using your connection to better understand and respond to what you read. One way of connecting is to think about the author's intentions. In this lesson, you will work to make connections and use them to understand what the author is saying to you, the reader.

Just as speeches and poems can persuade, *memoirs*—stories about peoples' lives—can be persuasive too. These stories illustrate issues that the author wants the reader to think about. *Farewell to Manzanar* was written by Jeanne Wakatsuki Houston, a Japanese American woman who was sent to live in internment camps during World War II.

In the excerpt below, Houston's family has just left the camps to return to "normal" American life. As you read about her return to school, consider what her story **persuades** you to think about. In your **Response Notes** record connections you make that persuade you to "listen" to her words.

from Farewell to Manzanar by Jeanne Wakatsuki Houston and James D. Houston

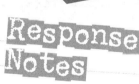

Response Notes

When the sixth-grade teacher ushered me in, the other kids inspected me, but not unlike I myself would study a new arrival. She was a warm, benevolent woman who tried to make this first day as easy as possible. She gave me the morning to get the feel of the room. That afternoon, during a reading lesson, she finally asked me if I'd care to try a page out loud. I had not yet opened my mouth, except to smile. When I stood up, everyone turned to watch. Any kid entering a new class wants, first of all, to be liked. This was uppermost in my mind. I smiled wider, then began to read. I made no mistakes. When I finished, a pretty blond girl in front of me said, quite innocently, "Gee, I didn't know you could speak English."

She was genuinely amazed. I was stunned. How could this have even been in doubt?

It isn't difficult, now, to explain her reaction. But at age eleven, I couldn't believe anyone could think such a thing, say such a thing about me, or regard me in that way. I smiled and sat down, suddenly aware of what being of Japanese ancestry was going to be like. I wouldn't be faced with physical attack, or with overt shows of hatred. Rather, I would be seen as someone foreign, or as someone other than American, or perhaps not be seen at all.

During the years in camp I had never really understood why we were there, nor had I questioned it much. I knew no one in my family had committed a crime. If I needed explanations at all, I conjured up vague notions about a *war* between America and Japan. But now I'd reached an age where certain childhood mysteries begin to make sense. This girl's guileless remark came as an illumination, an instant knowledge that brought with it the first buds of true shame.

From that day on, part of me yearned to be invisible. In a way, nothing would have been nicer than for no one to see me. Although I couldn't have defined it at the time, I felt that if attention were drawn to me, people would see what this girl had first responded to. They wouldn't see me, they would see the slant-eyed face, the Oriental. This is what accounts, in part, for the entire evacuation. You cannot deport 110,000 people unless you have stopped seeing individuals. ✤

✳ Take a moment to compare notes with a partner. Discuss the strongest connection you made to the text. Then fill in the chart below with thoughts about that connection.

Describe the connection you made.	How does this connection influence your response to the ideas presented in the text?

✳ What do you think Houston is trying to persuade us to think about?

_____

_____

_____

_____

> Make connections to a text to better understand your response to the author's viewpoint and beliefs.

In Unit 1, you took the approach of *Exploring Multiple Perspectives* when you read. You looked at a character's perspective, the author's perspective, and a historical perspective. Another way to explore multiple viewpoints is to examine different readers' responses. Readers respond differently to texts depending on their life experiences, beliefs, and connections. In this lesson, you'll examine how your own perspective influences your responses. And you'll examine how other readers' perspectives influence their responses.

In addition to nonfiction writing that **persuades** readers to think about an issue, fiction often does the same thing. The excerpt below, taken from *The Gold Cadillac* by Mildred D. Taylor, is told from the perspective of the narrator, a young girl nicknamed 'lois. As you read, consider what the author may be trying to **persuade** readers to think about. In your **Response Notes,** pay special attention to how your perspective influences your understanding and response to the story. Think about who you are and what connections you make to the text because of that perspective.

from **The Gold Cadillac** by Mildred D. Taylor

Response Notes

Though my mother didn't like the Cadillac, everybody else in the neighborhood certainly did. That meant quite a few folks too, since we lived on a very busy block. On one corner was a grocery store, a cleaner's, and a gas station. Across the street was a beauty shop and a fish market, and down the street was a bar, another grocery store, the Dixie Theater, the café, and a drugstore. There were always people strolling to or from one of these places and because our house was right in the middle of the block just about everybody had to pass our house and the gold Cadillac. Sometimes people took in the Cadillac as they walked, their heads turning for a longer look as they passed. Then there were people who just outright stopped and took a good look before continuing on their way. I was proud to say that car belonged to my family. I felt mighty important as people called to me as I ran down the street. "'Ey, 'lois! How's that Cadillac, girl? Riding fine?" I told my mother how much everybody liked that car. She was not impressed and made no comment.

Since just about everybody on the block knew everybody else, most folks knew that my mother wouldn't ride in the Cadillac. Because of that, my father took a lot of good-natured kidding from the men. My mother got kidded too as the women said if she didn't ride in that car, maybe some other woman would.

And everybody laughed about it and began to bet on who would give in first, my mother or my father. But then my father said he was going to drive the car south into Mississippi to visit my grandparents and everybody stopped laughing.

My uncles stopped.

So did my aunts.

Everybody.

"Look here, Wilbert," said one of my uncles, "it's too dangerous. It's like putting a loaded gun to your head."

"I paid good money for that car," said my father. "That gives me a right to drive it where I please. Even down to Mississippi."

My uncles argued with him and tried to talk him out of driving the car south. So did my aunts and so did the neighbors, Mr. LeRoy, Mr. Courtland, and Mr. Pondexter. They said it was a dangerous thing, a mighty dangerous thing, for a black man to drive an expensive car into the rural South.

"Not much those folks hate more'n to see a northern Negro coming down there in a fine car," said Mr. Pondexter. "They see those Ohio license plates, they'll figure you coming down uppity, trying to lord your fine car over them!"

I listened, but I didn't understand. I didn't understand why they didn't want my father to drive that car south. It was his.

"Listen to Pondexter, Wilbert!" cried another uncle. "We might've fought a war to free people overseas, but we're not free here! Man, those white folks down south'll lynch you soon's look at you. You know that!"

Wilma and I looked at each other. Neither one of us knew what *lynch* meant, but the word sent a shiver through us. We held each other's hand.

My father was silent, then he said: "All my life I've had to be heedful of what white folks thought. Well, I'm tired of that. I worked hard for everything I got. Got it honest, too. Now I got that Cadillac because I liked it and because it meant something to me that somebody like me from Mississippi could go and buy it. It's my car, I paid for it, and I'm driving it south."

My mother, who had said nothing through all this, now stood. "Then the girls and I'll be going too," she said.

"No!" said my father.

My mother only looked at him and went off to the kitchen.

My father shook his head. It seemed he didn't want us to go. My uncles looked at each other, then at my father. "You set on doing this, we'll all go," they said. "That way we can watch out for each other." My father took a moment and nodded. Then my aunts got up and went off to their kitchens too. ❖

✳ Through the use of a story, what do you think Taylor is persuading readers to think about? What makes you think so?

_____

_____

_____

_____

_____

✳ How does your perspective influence your response to the story? Do you feel fear for 'lois's family when they make the trip South? Tell why or why not. What new perspectives do you have on indifference or oppression from reading Taylor's story?

_____

_____

_____

_____

_____

✳ Compare what you've written with another classmate's responses. What differences did you notice? What similarities? Fill in the chart below to show how your different perspectives influenced your reading responses.

How your perspective influenced your reading response	How _____'s perspective influenced her/his reading response

Your life experiences, beliefs, and connections to the text shape your perspective on an issue.

Think about a time when you tried very hard to **persuade** someone about something. Chances are, you chose your language carefully. When authors write persuasively, they make careful language choices. They want to draw out from their readers the most powerful responses possible. And, as you've seen, they can choose to write in a variety of genres, such as speeches, poems, memoirs, or fictional stories.

In this unit, you've seen several examples of authors using various genres and different topics to take a stand against oppression and indifference. Now let's look at the language they chose to support their opinions. Use the chart below to analyze and compare how two different authors did this. Choose to compare Wiesel's speech with either Langston Hughes's poem or with Houston's memoir. Write the name of the piece at the top of the blank column on the right. You may need to skim the selections again and use your **Response Notes** to complete the chart.

Language and Craft	Elie Wiesel's speech, "The Perils of Indifference"	
Describe the *vocabulary* used. Does the author use "big" words or common words or both? Does the author use powerful words to get ideas across? Give examples. What is the effect of the vocabulary used?		
What is the *tone* the author uses (for example, serious, sad, sarcastic, funny)? Describe and give examples.		
Where and when did the author use *repetition* (repeating words or phrases)? What effect did it have on you?		
Did the selection convince you that it is important to stand up against oppression? Why or why not?		

✳ Which selection elicited the strongest reaction in you as a reader? Explain why, using specific details from the chart on the previous page to describe how the author's language and style prompted your response.

_____

_____

_____

_____

_____

_____

_____

✳ Explain what aspect of indifference or oppression the author persuaded you to think about. Describe how the author reinforced or changed your mind on the issue.

_____

_____

_____

_____

_____

_____

_____

_____

_____

_____

_____

Determine how language and style contribute to an author's ability to persuade you to consider his or her opinions and viewpoints.

Writers often write about what they know. Knowing about an author's life can help you understand the author's opinions and viewpoints. Of course, this doesn't mean that every book is an autobiography, or an author's account of his or her life. But writers borrow tidbits from their own lives or the lives of people they know to persuade others of their viewpoints.

As you read the following interview, pay special attention to the connections between Taylor's life and her viewpoints about oppression that are evident in *The Gold Cadillac*. You can reread the excerpt in Lesson 38. In your **Response Notes,** record the insights you have about the source of Taylor's ideas about indifference and oppression. Why do you think she became a writer?

Response Notes

from a interview with **Mildred D. Taylor**

"From as far back as I can remember my father taught me a different history from the one I learned in school. By the fireside in our Ohio home and in Mississippi, where I was born and where my father's family had lived since the days of slavery, I had heard about our past. It was not an organized history beginning in a certain year, but one told through stories about great-grandparents and aunts and uncles and others that stretched back through the years of slavery and beyond. It was a history of ordinary people. Some brave, some not so brave, but basically people who had done nothing more spectacular than survive in a society designed for their destruction. Some of the stories my father had learned from his parents and grandparents as they had learned from theirs; others he told first-hand, having been involved in the incidents himself. There was often humor in his stories, sometimes pathos, and frequently tragedy; but always the people were graced with a simple dignity that elevated them from the ordinary to the heroic.

"Those colorful vignettes stirred the romantic in me. I was fascinated by the stories, not only because of what they said or because they were about my family, but because of the manner in which my father told them. I began to imagine myself as storyteller, making people laugh at their own human foibles or nod their heads with pride about some stunning feat of heroism. But I was a shy and quiet child, so I turned to creating stories for myself instead, carving elaborate daydreams in my mind.

"I do not know how old I was when the daydreams became more than that, and I decided to write them down, but by the time I entered high school, I was confident that I would one day be a writer. I still wonder at myself for feeling so confident since I had never particularly liked to write, nor was I exceptionally good at it. But once I had made up my mind to write, I had no doubts about doing it. It was just something that would one day be. I had always been taught that I could achieve anything I set my mind to. Still a number of years were to lapse before this setting of my mind actually resulted in the publication of any of my stories.

"In those intervening years spent studying, traveling, and living in Africa, and working with the Black student movement, I would find myself turning again and again to the stories I had heard in my childhood." ❖

❋ Now that you've read Mildred Taylor's words, you have additional information about her viewpoints. Based on your perspective, experiences, and what you have read, what would you say to persuade students to stand up against oppression? Write a draft of the speech you would give. Be as creative as you'd like, and draw on what Taylor says in the interview and in the excerpt from *The Gold Cadillac* that you read.

Speech About Standing Up Against Oppression

✳ Do you have the power to persuade someone? First decide what you want to convince someone else to consider from one of the pieces you've read. Choose the issue and write a few sentences describing why it is important to you.

_____

_____

_____

_____

✳ Brainstorm a list of details and examples that will help you persuade someone to agree with you.

Details to Convince

Examples to Convince

The Topic

Issues to Consider

✳ Write a paragraph that is as persuasive as you can make it. Convince your readers to think about your point of view on the issue.

_____

_____

_____

_____

_____

_____

_____

_____

Determine what an author wants to persuade you to believe and how convincingly he or she presents the issues and point of view.

Interacting with the Text

Q What do these two questions have in common?

What are the three tallest buildings in the world? and *Which has more grams of fat—a hamburger, a chicken burger, or a muffin?*

A You can better display the answers in pictures than in words.

Writers sometimes use visual texts such as graphs, diagrams, and illustrations to pack a lot of information into a small amount of space and to give information more clearly.

In this unit, you will travel to ancient Egypt where you will learn about topics that have fascinated people for centuries. In the process, you will learn to get important **information** from visual texts and to create effective visual texts of your own.

When they want to compare different amounts, writers often use graphs. You can use a bar graph to show the amount of fat in different foods, for example. You would set up a **bar graph** like this:

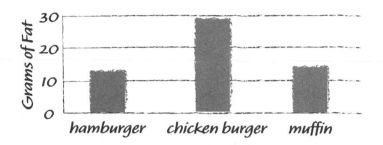

A pictograph is another kind of graph that uses symbols or pictures rather than bars. As you read the first paragraph of the excerpt below, try to **visualize** the height of the Great Pyramid. In the **Response Notes**, sketch symbols or pictures you could use in a pictograph.

"Famous Pyramids" from *Egyptian Pyramids* by Anne Steel

Response Notes

The earliest Egyptian graves were very simple and could easily be broken into and robbed. To prevent this, the Egyptians began to build tombs called mastabas. These were rectangular buildings placed over a burial chamber. Pharaohs had mastabas built with many rooms inside to protect the burial chamber from thieves, but the graves were still robbed.

The first pyramid was built for Pharaoh Zoser at Sakkara. There were six huge steps built on top of the tomb to make it safer from robbers. The Pharaoh's spirit was believed to have climbed the steps of the pyramid to the stars. Later pyramids were built without steps, like the famous group at Giza. The largest of these is the Great Pyramid, built for Pharaoh Khufu. Each side is 450 feet (144 m) high and measures 756 feet (230 m) at the base. It would have taken at least twenty years to build. ❖

✳ Does the Great Pyramid seem very tall to you? What evidence is there in the text?

Now there are other buildings taller than the Great Pyramid. But for 4,000 years, it was the tallest structure in the world. Anne Steel gave its current size of 450 feet, but when it was built, it was 31 feet (9.5 m) taller. The creator of the pictograph that follows claims that the pyramid is 449.5 feet high and rounds that number down for the graphic. Read the pictograph and answer the questions that follow.

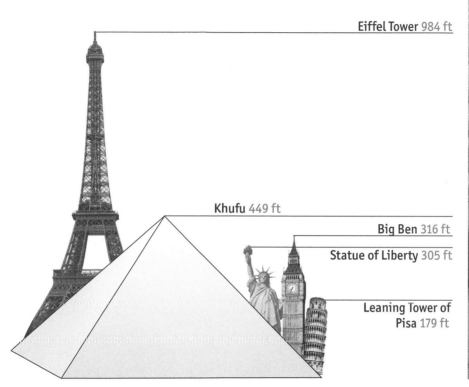

Eiffel Tower 984 ft

Khufu 449 ft

Big Ben 316 ft

Statue of Liberty 305 ft

Leaning Tower of Pisa 179 ft

✳ Which building is taller than the Great Pyramid?

✳ How much taller is it?

✳ Which is taller—the Statue of Liberty or the Leaning Tower of Pisa?

✳ Is it easier or harder to read the graph instead of the words? Explain.

✳ Create your own pictograph to display information. You can use information that is familiar to you, such as the height of people in your family. You can do some research on tall buildings to find other comparisons to the Great Pyramid. Or you can look for information on a topic you are studying in science or social studies.

Pictographs and bar graphs are useful when a writer wants to show or compare different amounts.

A **diagram** is another kind of visual text. Diagrams may show the parts of something, or they may show how something works. If you have background knowledge about a topic, a diagram might give you more information. In this lesson, you will read background information about building the pyramids before you look at the parts of the pyramid.

When you read in Lesson 41 that the Great Pyramid took at least twenty years to build, did you wonder why? One reason is that pyramids were very complex structures, with a lot of rooms and passageways. As you read the next section from *Egyptian Pyramids*, circle words and phrases that show how difficult it was to build the pyramids.

"The Pyramid Builders" from *Egyptian Pyramids* by Anne Steel

Response Notes

Many thousands of people were needed to build a pyramid. Some of them, such as the architect and planners, were highly skilled. Their plans had to be accepted by the pharaoh before any work could begin. Quarry men were needed to get the stone out of the ground, and masons worked to shape the rough stone. Painters decorated the walls inside the tomb, and sculptors made statues and carvings.

The heavy work of moving the stones was done by people with no special building skills. Some of them were farmers who had to leave their land for some time each year when the Nile flooded. Others may have been prisoners, or people paying labor tax to the pharaoh. As there was no money in Ancient Egypt, the workers were paid with food, wine, clothes, and other goods.

Review the words or phrases you circled. Make a note of two important facts that you learned from this excerpt.

✳ Use the notes you made in Lesson 41 and the two facts you just wrote to write a summary of the excerpts from *Egyptian Pyramids*. Restate the main idea in your own words. Include some of the most important facts you have learned to give details about the main idea.

_____

_____

_____

_____

_____

_____

_____

_____

❋ Diagrams often go with printed text. Look at the diagram of the pyramid below. As you read the excerpt that goes with it, use colored markers to match the parts of the diagram to the sentences that describe those parts.

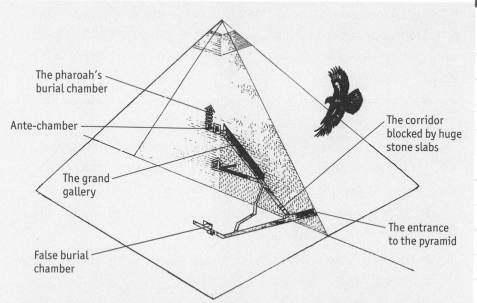

The pharoah's burial chamber

Ante-chamber

The grand gallery

False burial chamber

The corridor blocked by huge stone slabs

The entrance to the pyramid

Inside, the pyramid was a maze of passages and rooms. The main aim of the builders was to hide the burial chambers so that thieves could not steal its treasures. The entrance was usually on the north side of the pyramid and it was always well hidden. Inside, the passages might lead to false burial chambers or dead ends. In the Great Pyramid there was a false chamber underground. The real chamber was blocked off with huge stone slabs. But this was not enough to keep robbers from stealing everything except the stone tomb. ❖

❋ Did the diagram help you visualize? Did the diagram help you understand pyramids better? Why or why not?

_____

_____

_____

_____

_____

_____

Diagrams can help a reader see the parts of something or understand how things work.

If you've ever had to write a research report, you probably read about your topic in several different places, such as reference books, magazine articles, and the Internet. But how did you keep track of all that information? One way to organize your information is by **taking notes** as you read. Some people use a combination of words and pictures to take notes; some just use words. Here are a few tips about note-taking:

- Notes do not need to be in complete sentences. You can jot down words or phrases.

- There is no one right way to take notes. Some people make formal outlines or lists, while other people use webs or other graphic organizers. Pick a style that works for you.

- Don't take notes about everything that you read. Write only the most important ideas.

- Organize your notes with headings, titles, or whatever system works for you.

- Use numbers, symbols, and/or abbreviations to help you take notes more quickly.

Imagine that you are an archaeologist, studying one of the most fascinating topics in ancient Egypt—mummies. As you read the excerpt, jot down comments and questions in the **Response Notes.** Remember that you can use words, pictures, or symbols for your notes.

from **The Ancient Egyptians** by Elsa Marston

Why did the ancient Egyptians mummify their dead? The procedure was an essential part of their belief in the afterlife. For a person to enjoy eternal life, his or her body had to be preserved.

The Egyptians probably got the idea by observing that desert sands would sometimes dry and preserve a body naturally. Then they learned how to mummify artificially. Though at first only the royal and rich had the privilege of being preserved, later almost everyone but the very poor expected to be mummified. There were different grades of mummification, from the quick, cheap job to the full seventy days' treatment for kings.

The first step in mummification was to take out most of the internal organs and preserve them. The heart was left in the body to be weighed by the gods; the brain, though, was discarded because it was not thought to be of any value. After being immersed for many days in a special kind of salt called natron, the body was treated with special ointments and finally wrapped carefully in long strips of linen. The mummification business was always a thriving one, and it lasted well into Roman times. ✦

✳ Using a graphic organizer can help you keep track of information. Review the notes you made. Then use this sequence map to list the steps involved in mummification.

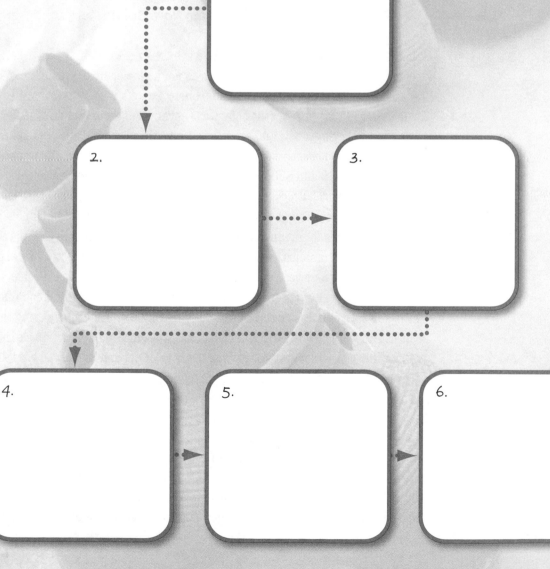

1. Internal organs were taken out and preserved.

2.

3.

4.

5.

6.

Greenland ★

Ireland ★

★ Italy

✳ Although Egypt is the best-known location of mummies, they have also been found in other parts of the world. Look at the map and think about how those mummies might have been made.

✳ Talk with a partner about the map. Looking at it, and using what you know about geography, discuss whether you think all mummies were made the same way. Read "Accidental Mummies" to find out.

"Accidental Mummies" from *Nova* Online

Some of the most spectacular mummies were created accidentally. In 1991, German climbers found a body frozen on top of a glacier near the Austrian-Italian border. Initially, the police and forensic experts who arrived on the scene didn't realize how old the body was—even though he was wearing a grass cape, carrying a bow and arrows and had shoes stuffed with grass for warmth. Later, radiocarbon dating determined that the "Iceman" died sometime between 3350 and 3300 B.C.—making him the oldest well-preserved mummy in the world.

In 1972, hunters found some of the best naturally-preserved human bodies at a remarkable abandoned settlement called Qilakitsoq, in Greenland. The "Greenland Mummies," who died about 500 years ago, consisted of a six-month old baby, a four-year-old boy, and six women of various ages. Protected by a rock that overhung a shallow cave, the bodies were naturally mummified by the sub-zero temperatures and dry, dehydrating winds. Accompanying the eight bodies were seventy-eight items of clothing, most made out of sealskin.

Over the years, peat cutters working the bogs of northwest Europe have uncovered hundreds of mummies. The spongy top layer of a peat bog tends to seal off oxygen from the layers below. A bog's naturally acidic environment also helps to create mummies and gives them a distinctively brown, leathery and life-like appearance. The oldest "bog mummies" are from the Iron Age (between 400 B.C. and 400 A.D.) and were Celtic or Germanic contemporaries of the Romans. Strangely, many of the mummies found in the European bogs show evidence of violent deaths. With slit throats and broken skulls, these individuals may have been victims of ritual sacrifice, not unlike the mummies of the high Andes. ✤

✳ Use a chart when you need to sort information into categories. Imagine that you are going to write a report on different ways that people have been mummified. Look over the information in this lesson. Make notes in the boxes below.

	Egypt	Greenland	Northwest Europe
What was used to dry or preserve the bodies?	First sand, then salt		
When were people mummified?	"ancient"— check the years		
Why were people mummified?		Accident?	
Who was mummified?			Maybe human sacrifices

✳ Using the information from the chart, write one paragraph that could be a part of your report on mummies. You can use one of the questions in the chart as your first sentence or you can write a different one.

_____

_____

_____

_____

_____

_____

_____

Taking notes helps readers and writers organize information and communicate important ideas.

READING AN ILLUSTRATION

You have probably heard that "a picture is worth a thousand words." Authors of informational texts know this. They often use photos and illustrations to emphasize key points or to make an important point. When the subject is unfamiliar, an illustration can help you better understand what you are reading. In fact, a good way to preview what you are going to read is to look at the illustrations.

Did you know that the ancient Egyptians mummified animals as well as humans? In this lesson, you will read about one type of animal mummy—cats. The following picture comes from the book *Cat Mummies.* Look at it for several minutes. Write your questions or reactions in the **Response Notes.**

Response Notes

✳ Talk with one or two other students about your observations. Write two questions that you still have.

Laszlo Kubinyi drew the illustration on page 142 to accompany a description of how cats were mummified. Read the description.

from Cat Mummies by Kelly Trumble

Sometimes a cat was mummified in an elaborate way. The body was wrapped in strips of linen that had been dyed in two colors. The linen strips were woven together to form beautiful patterns. The head was covered with a mask made of a material similar to papier-mâché. Pieces of linen were sewn on the mask to look like eyes. Ears were made from the midribs of palm leaves, set in a natural position.

Other cats were mummified in a simple way. They were rolled up only in a piece of plain linen. But the rolling was done with the care and respect that a sacred animal deserved. ❖

❋ Did this passage answer more of your questions? If so, go back and write the answers by your questions. Circle any questions you still have.

❋ Illustrations often set a tone for the information. When you see the picture, you get a certain feeling about the subject. Look again at the illustration of the cat mummies. What feeling does it give you? What mood does it suggest? Common words for mood are *scary, exciting, tense, calm, funny,* and so on. Write one or two words here that you think fit the picture and tell why.

_____

_____

❋ Do you think that the illustration better fits the *information* in the excerpt by Kelly Trumble or the *mood*? Explain.

_____

_____

_____

_____

_____

_____

_____

_____

Illustrations emphasize information in a text or add new information. They can also set the mood or tone of informational text.

LESSON 45 — READING A WEBSITE

Websites can be good sources of factual information if you know how to read them. Perhaps you still have unanswered questions about mummies or ancient Egyptians. Perhaps you just want to learn more about them. Or maybe you have a big report coming up, and you have decided to write about some aspect of ancient Egypt. You need to know more.

A website consists of pages and links. The links allow you to explore a subject in greater detail. You can preview the website by looking at the links, pictures, and icons. You want to know whether it has the information you need. Let's say you do have questions about animal mummies. Look at the web page to see if it would be helpful.

When you click on the link "Egyptian Mummies" you find another link to "Egyptian Animal Mummies." Read the article and see if it answers any of your questions.

Websites have lots of information, but you have to be sure the information is accurate. Ask yourself questions such as these to **evaluate a website:** Is the source of the site legitimate and well known? Are the people who contribute to the page knowledgeable? What is the purpose of the website? When was the site last updated? Can the information be verified by another source? The answers to these questions should tell you whether you can trust a website.

"The Kittens of Egypt" by James M. Deem

Mummies come in all shapes and sizes—and species. The ancient Egyptians mummified reptiles and animals such as dogs, apes, bulls, rams, and even an occasional hippopotamus. However, one of the most common animal mummies in Egypt was the cat. To determine how, when, and why cats were mummified, Egyptologists have had to piece together many clues. It appears, for example, that by 1350 B.C., cats were occasionally buried with their owners, according to author Jaromir Malek.

But by 900 B.C., a striking change had taken place in the Egyptians' religious beliefs. Many animals were now thought to be the embodiment of certain gods and goddesses; cats were believed to represent the goddess Bastet. Consequently, they were raised in and around temples devoted to Bastet. When they died, they were mummified and buried in huge cemeteries, often in large communal graves.

An even more important change took place over the centuries. From about 332 B.C. to 30 B.C., animals began to be raised for the specific purpose of being turned into mummies. The mummies were sold to people on their way to worship a god and left at the temple as offerings. Scientists have uncovered a gruesome fact: many cats died quite premature and unnatural deaths. Two-to four-month-old kittens seemed to have been sacrificed in huge numbers, perhaps, as Malek supposes, because they fit into the mummy container better. So many cat mummies were made that researchers can only guess that there were millions of them. In fact, one company bought 38,000 pounds of cat mummies in the late 1800s to pulverize and sell as fertilizer in England; this shipment alone probably contained 180,000 mummified cats. ❖

✳ What three things did you learn from this article? What questions does it answer? What new questions do you have? Talk with one or two other students to get your questions answered. Write two or three important points from your discussion.

_____

_____

_____

_____

_____

✳ Apply what you know about using visual texts. Select one written text from this unit. Design a visual that will go with that text and provide information at a glance. Of course, if the piece already has a visual text, such as a diagram or a pictograph, give it a different treatment, such as an illustration or a graphic organizer.

Selection Title: _____

✳ Explain why you chose to use the visual text that you did.

_____
_____
_____
_____
_____
_____
_____
_____
_____
_____
_____
_____

Understanding how to read websites is important for finding useful information.

Making Connections

Imagine this: A dance group visits your school to do a performance of merengue, a type of dance that began in the Dominican Republic. Two weeks later, you attend your uncle's wedding. At the reception, you make a connection—you hear music that sounds like the music from the merengue performance at your school. You say to your cousin, "That reminds me of the merengue performance at school. Let me tell you about it."

When you read, you connect what you are thinking or remembering to the text you are reading. Connections like this can also give you ideas for writing. In this unit, you will work at connecting what you read to your life, to movies, to books, or to others' stories, events, or situations. Notice how **making connections** can influence your reading.

147

46

CONNECTING THE TEXT TO YOURSELF

As we discussed in previous units, it is important to **make connections** between what you are reading and what you know and have experienced. For example, something you read might make you remember a similar experience or feeling you've had. These kinds of connections can help you relate to the story, even if the characters seem very different from you. "To relate" means that you understand or feel involved or concerned about the situation or the characters.

Sometimes the connections come easily. Other times it can be difficult to make them. Take time to think about and find connections even when they don't come easily. The more connections you make, the more personal meaning you will find in what you read.

The following excerpt is from Zilpha Keatley Snyder's novel, *The Egypt Game*. It is about friendship and imagination, and has a sprinkling of history and mystery. In the **Response Notes,** make notes about connections you make to your life experiences.

from **The Egypt Game** by Zilpha Keatley Snyder

Response Notes

On that same day in August, just a few minutes before twelve, Melanie Ross arrived at the door of Mrs. Hall's apartment on the third floor. Melanie was eleven years old and she had lived in the Casa Rosada since she was only seven. During that time she'd welcomed a lot of new people to the apartment house. Apartment dwellers, particularly near a university, are apt to come and go. Melanie always looked forward to meeting new tenants, and today was going to be especially interesting. Today, Melanie had been sent up to get Mrs. Hall's granddaughter to come down and have lunch with the Rosses. Melanie didn't know much about the new girl except that her name was April and that she had come from Hollywood to live with Mrs. Hall, who was her grandmother.

It would be neat if she turned out to be a real friend. There hadn't been any girls the right age in the Casa Rosada lately. To have a handy friend again, for spur-of-the moment visiting, would be great. However, she had overheard something that didn't sound too promising. Just the other day she'd heard Mrs. Hall telling Mom that April was a strange little thing because she'd been brought up all over everywhere and never had much of a chance to associate with other children. You wouldn't know what to expect of someone like that. But then, you never knew what to expect of any new kid, not really. So Melanie knocked hopefully at the door of apartment 312.

Meeting people had always been easy for Melanie. Most people she liked right away, and they usually seemed to feel the same way about her. But when the door to 312 opened that morning, for just a moment she was almost speechless. Surprise can do that to a person, and at first glance April really was a surprise. Her hair was stacked up in a pile that seemed to be more pins than hair, and the whole thing teetered forward over her thin pale face. She was wearing a big, yellowish-white fur thing around her shoulders, and carrying a plastic purse almost as big as a suitcase. But most of all it was the eyelashes. They were black and bushy looking, and the ones on her left eye were higher up and sloped in a different direction. Melanie's mouth opened and closed a few times before anything came out.

✳ What connections can you make to the story? If you have difficulty, pause and think about what you read. In what ways do the characters or the feelings or the situation seem familiar to you?

_____

_____

_____

✳ In the next excerpt, which takes place on the same day, Melanie and April have just finished playing an imaginative story-telling game. Continue reading and jotting down connections you make to your life experiences.

As they walked to the door Melanie asked, "Do you want to play some more tomorrow?"

April was adjusting her fur stole around her shoulders for the trip upstairs. "Oh, I guess so," she said with a sudden return to haughtiness.

But Melanie was beginning to understand about April's frozen spells, and how to thaw her out. You just had to let her know she couldn't make you stop liking her that easily. "None of my friends know how to play imagining games the way you do," Melanie said. "Some of them can do it a little bit but they mostly don't have any very good ideas. And a lot of them only like ball games or other things that are already made up. But I like imagining games better than anything."

April was being very busy trying to get her stole to stay on because the clasp was a little bit broken. All at once she pulled it off, wadded it all up and tucked it under her arm. She looked right straight at Melanie and said, "You know what? I never did call them that before, but imagining games are just about all I ever play because most of the time I never have anybody to play with."

She started off up the hall. Then she turned around and walked backward, waving her fur stole around her head like a lasso. "You've got lots of good ideas, too," she yelled. ❖

✳ Share and compare your **Response Notes** with a partner's. Have your partner help you choose your strongest connection. In your conversation, explain the connection by telling the story you were reminded of while reading this one. That's how many ideas for stories are formed—by reflecting on life stories and connections. Below, write the story behind the connection, as if you were telling it to a friend.

_____

_____

_____

_____

_____

_____

_____

_____

_____

_____

_____

_____

_____

_____

_____

_____

_____

_____

Connecting life experiences to the text helps readers relate to and become involved in what they are reading. These connections also offer ideas for writing.

47 LESSON

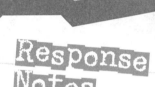

In earlier units of the *Daybook*, you made connections to another text, such as a book or short story, a movie, a piece of artwork, a poem, or a song. Somehow the texts are related, but your mind begins to wonder how and why. You ask yourself, "How are they the same? How are they different? How does one text help me understand the other?" Often, you make the connections in the back of your mind without really noticing.

In this lesson, you're going to practice noticing what connections you make while you read. Read the following excerpt, also from Zilpha Keatley Snyder's novel *The Egypt Game*. Note that Caroline is April's grandmother and Marshall is Melanie's little brother. In the **Response Notes,** record connections you make to other texts.

from **The Egypt Game** by Zilpha Keatley Snyder

Response Notes

All through the month of August, Melanie and April were together almost every day. They played the paper-families game and other games, both in the Rosses' apartment and in Caroline's. They took Marshall for walks and to the park while Mrs. Ross was gone to her class, and almost every day they went to the library. It was in the library in August that the seeds were planted that grew into the Egypt Game in September in Professor's deserted yard.

It all started when April found a new book about Egypt, an especially interesting one about the life of a young pharaoh. She passed it on to Melanie, and with it a lot of her interest in all sorts of ancient stuff. Melanie was soon as fascinated by the valley of the Nile as April had been. Before long, with the help of a sympathetic librarian, they had found and read just about everything the library had to offer on Egypt—both fact and fiction.

They read about Egypt in the library during the day, and at home in the evening, and in bed late at night when they were supposed to be asleep. Then in the mornings while they helped each other with their chores they discussed the things they had found out. In a very short time they had accumulated all sorts of fascinating facts about tombs and temples, pharaohs and pyramids, mummies and monoliths, and dozens of other exotic topics. They decided that the Egyptians couldn't have been more interesting if they had done it on purpose. Everything, from their love of beauty and mystery, to their fascinating habit of getting married when they were only eleven years old, made good stuff to talk about. By the end of the month, April and Melanie were beginning work on their own alphabet of hieroglyphics for writing secret messages, and at the library they were beginning to be called the Egypt Girls.

But in between all the good times, both April and Melanie were spending some bad moments worrying about the beginning of school. April was worried because she knew from experience—lots of it—that it isn't easy to face a new class in a new school. She didn't admit it, not even to Melanie, but she was having nightmares about the first day of school. There were classroom nightmares, and schoolyard nightmares and principal's office nightmares. ❖

✳ Using the connections you made, fill in the following Connections Chart.

This part of *The Egypt Game* . . .	reminded me of this other text . . .	because . . .

✳ Compare your Connections Chart with a partner's and discuss the types of connections you each made.

✳ Now describe the strongest connection you made. Was the other text a song, picture, movie, or another book? What was the subject of the connection? How did the connection make you feel? Explain.

_____

_____

_____

_____

_____

Comparing texts helps you make your reading more meaningful.

As they read, good readers make connections to things they know. Sometimes readers come across situations about which they know little or nothing. What happens then? One way to connect to unfamiliar experiences and places is to ask questions such as these: Why would a person act that way? What would life be like if I lived in this place with these rules? What would I do if I were in that position? Take time to think about and ask questions that help you connect to the issues, the people, and the events in what you read.

In the following excerpt, April, Melanie, and Marshall have been playing "The Egypt Game" that they created. In the **Response Notes,** make connections by asking questions about what is unfamiliar to you or what makes you curious.

from **The Egypt Game** by Zilpha Keatley Snyder

Response Notes

...Nobody ever planned [the Egypt Game] ahead, at least, not very far. Ideas began and grew and afterwards it was hard to remember just how. That was one of the mysterious and fascinating things about it.

On that particular day, the game about Marshamosis, the boy pharaoh, and Set, the god of evil, didn't get very far. They'd no more than gotten started when April and Melanie decided they just had to have some more equipment before they could play it well. So they postponed the game and went instead to scout around in the alley for boards and boxes to use in making things like thrones and altars. They found just what they needed behind the doughnut shop and the furniture store in the next block, and brought them back to Egypt. And it was on the same trip that they had the good luck to rescue an old metal mixing bowl from a garbage pail. April said it would be just the thing for a firepit for building sacred fires.

When they had everything as far as the hole in the fence, they ran into a problem. The bowl and boards went through all right, but the boxes were just too big. The only solution was to throw them over the top of the fence. It wasn't easy, and in landing they made quite a bit of noise.

It wasn't long afterwards that the curtain on the small window at the back of the Professor's store was pushed very carefully to one side. But April and Melanie were so busy building and planning that they didn't notice at all. Only someone with very sharp eyes would have been able to see the figure that stood silently behind the very dirty window in the darkened room.

...That was about where they were in the Game, when something happened that almost put an end to the Egypt Game; and not to the Egypt Game alone, but to all the outdoor games in the whole neighborhood. On that particular afternoon, the girls had built a dungeon out of cardboard boxes in the corner of the storage yard. Elizabeth and Marshall were languishing in the dungeon, tied hand and foot, victims of the priests of Set. April and Melanie were creeping cautiously from pillar to pillar in the Temple of Evil, on their way to the rescue. Melanie was crouching behind an imaginary pillar, when suddenly she straightened up and stood listening. In the dungeon Elizabeth heard it too, and quickly untied her bonds. April ran to help Marshall with his. They were really only kite string and knotted easily. From somewhere not too far away, perhaps the main alley behind the Casa Rosada, Mrs. Ross's voice was calling, "Melanie! Marshall! Melanie!" There was something about the tone of her voice that made Melanie's eyes widen with fear.

"Something's wrong," she said.

"It's too early," April nodded. "She never gets home this early."

They scrambled through the hole in the fence and, dragging Marshall to hurry him up, they dashed for the main alley behind the Casa Rosada. From there they could safely answer without giving the location of Egypt away.

Mrs. Ross met them near the back door of the apartment house. Even though they all clamored to know what was the matter, she only shook her head and said, "There's been some trouble in the neighborhood. April, you and Elizabeth come up to our apartment until your folks get home."

Of course they were all terribly curious, but Mrs. Ross wouldn't say any more. "We'll wait to discuss it until we have the facts," she said. "What I know right now amounts only to rumors. There may not be any truth in the story at all."

It occurred to all of them, though, that the rumors had been frightening enough to make Mrs. Ross cancel her after-school remedial reading class—which she almost never did—and come home early. And Melanie noticed a strangeness in her voice and that her hand shook as she put milk and cookies on the table. It had to be something serious. ❖

✻ Compare your **Response Notes** with a partner's. Discuss the questions you asked. Add any new questions that arise from your conversation.

✳ Choose one of the questions and try to answer it. Describe how your question and possible answer help you make sense of the story.

_____

_____

_____

_____

_____

_____

_____

_____

_____

✳ REFLECT: Take a moment to think about the three kinds of connections you've made in this unit: connecting text to yourself; connecting text to other texts; and connecting text to big questions. For you, which type seems to come most easily with *The Egypt Game* excerpts? Why do you think so? Write about it below.

_____

_____

_____

_____

_____

_____

_____

_____

_____

_____

_____

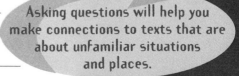

Asking questions will help you make connections to texts that are about unfamiliar situations and places.

Think about the earlier example of hearing music at your cousin's wedding, connecting it to a merengue performance you saw, then using that experience to describe the merengue to your cousin. That's what you're going to practice here; not dancing, of course, but using the connections you make to the text.

If a character experiences something that reminds you of something you've experienced, ask yourself, "How does that connection help me better understand what I'm reading?" The answer might be that you can feel what the character feels. If the setting in something you read reminds you of the setting in a movie you saw, you might be able to better understand what you're reading because you can picture it so clearly. If something you read reminds you of something you heard on the news, you might be able to better understand the situation by asking questions about why both of these things happen.

The excerpt you are about to read is from Linda Sue Park's *Project Mulberry,* a novel about family, friendship, and what it means to "be American." In the **Response Notes,** record connections you make as you read. Afterwards, you'll reflect on how those connections help you understand the text better.

Response Notes

from **Project Mulberry** by Linda Sue Park

Patrick and I became friends because of a vegetable.

Not just any vegetable.

A cabbage.

And not just any old cabbage. A Korean pickled cabbage. Which isn't a round cabbage like Peter Rabbit would eat, but a longer, leafier kind. It gets cut up and salted and packed in big jars with lots of garlic, green onions, and hot red pepper, and then it's called *kimchee.* Kimchee is really spicy. Koreans eat it for breakfast, lunch, and dinner.

I don't like kimchee. My mom says that when I was little, I used to eat it. She'd rinse off the spiciness and give me a bite or two. When I got to be six or seven years old, she stopped rinsing it. Most Korean mothers do that, and most Korean kids keep eating it.

Not me. I hated the spiciness, and I still do. My mom keeps telling me I should eat it because it's refreshing. But what's so refreshing about having your mouth on fire?

My family used to tease me about not liking kimchee. My dad said maybe it meant I wasn't really Korean. "We should have your DNA tested," he'd tell me. The seven-year-old snotbrain named Kenny who lives with us—otherwise known as my little brother—would wave big pieces in front of me and threaten to force me to eat them.

Another thing about kimchee is, it has a really strong smell. Even though it's stored in jars, you can still smell it, right through the jar and the refrigerator door. It sends out these feelers through the whole house.

Three years ago, when I was in fourth grade, we were living in Chicago. I'd made friends with a girl named Sarah. The first time she came over to play, she stopped dead in the entryway and said, "*Eww!* What's that smell?"

I'd never really noticed it. Smells are funny that way—they can sort of disappear if you live with them all the time. But Sarah was so grossed out that I was really embarrassed.

The exact same thing happened again a few weeks later, this time with two friends, a boy named Michael and his sister, Lily. They *both* stopped dead in their tracks and grabbed their noses. They insisted that we play outside because they couldn't stand the smell.

I asked my mom to stop making kimchee, but she told me I was being unreasonable.

When we moved to Plainfield two years ago, our new apartment didn't smell like kimchee—for about half a day. Then my mom unpacked some groceries, including a big jar of kimchee. *Sigh.* ✣

Review your **Response Notes** to help you determine the strogest connection you made so far. Describe that connection and how it helps you to better understand the story or influences your response to the story.

Describe a connection you made	How does the connection enhance your understanding of the story?

Response Notes

In *Project Mulberry,* the author, Linda Sue Park, inserts an imaginary dialogue between herself and the main character, Julia. It is a technique authors sometimes use to develop the personalities and voices of their characters or to reveal more about themselves. Here's how the story within a story begins:

Every story has another story inside, but you don't usually get to read the inside one. It's deleted or torn up or maybe filed away before the story becomes a book; lots of times it doesn't even get written down in the first place. If you'd rather read my story without interruption, you can skip these sections. Really and truly. I hereby give you official permission.

But if you're interested in learning about how this book was written—background information, mistakes, maybe even a secret or two—you've come to the right place. Some people like that sort of thing. It's mostly conversations between me and the author, Ms. Park. We had a lot of discussions while she was writing. ❖

✳ Read the following excerpts from the dialogue, and take notes about the connections you make between this text and the excerpt you read earlier.

Ms. Park: ...I hated kimchee when I was little. I like it now, but I didn't when I was your age.

Me: Wow. You can remember that far back?

Ms. Park: Very funny. I don't remember everything, of course. But parts of my childhood are quite vivid to me, and I like going there in my mind. You probably will, too, when you're older.

Me: Did your parents grow up in Korea?

Ms. Park: Yes. And my father always did the dishes.

Me: Did you have a bratty younger brother? Is that why you put Kenny in the story?

Ms. Park: I have a younger brother and a younger sister. But neither of them was very bratty. I got along with them pretty well when we were kids.

Me: A sister would be *much* better... ❖

✳ In what way does the excerpt you read earlier influence your understanding of this excerpt?

_____

_____

_____

_____

_____

_____

_____

_____

_____

✳ Write a dialogue with yourself that retells or explains a memorable event when you were younger. Choose an event that makes a strong connection to the person you have become.

_____

_____

_____

_____

_____

_____

_____

_____

Using the connections you make can help you better understand and remember the text you are reading.

Often the connections you make influence how you respond to what you read. Think back to the merengue example just once more. Imagine that you absolutely loved the performance you saw. That connection to the music at the wedding might make you respond with pleasure because you are hearing it again. It might inspire you and make you want to dance. When you're reading, the connections you make can help elicit your emotional (how you feel) and intellectual (what your brain thinks) responses.

If, for example, you learned about General Trujillo in Social Studies class, that connection to the plot of *Before We Were Free* (in the first unit in this book) might influence your response to what happens to Anita's family. Or, if you could relate to April in *The Egypt Game,* when she said she rarely had anyone to play with, your response to her odd actions might be very sympathetic.

Read the next excerpt from *Project Mulberry.* In the **Response Notes,** record connections you make as you read. After, you'll reflect on how those connections influence your response to the text.

from **Project Mulberry** by Linda Sue Park

Response Notes

I met Patrick on our second day in Plainfield, a Saturday morning. Actually, I saw him on the first day; he was hanging around on his front steps three doors down, watching the movers. Him and his three brothers as well. I noticed him right away, not because of the way he looked—brown hair in a normal boy-haircut, a few freckles, a gap between his front teeth that predicted braces in his future—but because he seemed to be the closest to my age. The other three boys were little, younger even than Kenny.

On the second day, I took a break from unpacking and went out to have a good look at our neighborhood. There they were again, the four boys, like they'd never moved off the steps. This time there was a girl with them, too, but she was a lot older.

Patrick came down the steps and said hello and told me his name. I said hi back and told him mine.

"Can I see inside your house?" he asked.

"Sure," I said.

...As we walked in the door of my house, Patrick tilted his head and sniffed. I braced myself for his reaction.

"Whoa," he said. "What's that? It smells great!"

That was the beginning of Patrick's love affair with kimchee. Whenever he eats dinner with us, my mom puts one bowl of kimchee on the table for the family and gives Patrick a whole private bowl for himself. He eats it in huge mouthfuls, sometimes without even adding any rice. I can hardly stand to watch him.

Maybe he's the one who needs his DNA tested. ❖

✳ With a partner, discuss the connections you made and how they influence your response to the story.

Describe a connection you made	How does the connection influence your response to the story?

✳ Take a moment to reflect on the different kinds of connections you made while reading *Project Mulberry*. Remember, you can make connections to yourself (what you know or have experienced), to other texts (including movies, art, and music), and to unfamiliar situations. Write about what you think is important in the story and explain why you think so.

_____

_____

_____

_____

_____

_____

_____

_____

✳ Create a graphic or visual representation that reminds you of the types of connections you can make while reading.

The connections you make can influence your response to what you read.

Exploring Multiple Perspectives

Have you seen athletes argue with the officials, fans, or other players? Do you sometimes argue with your friends or your parents? Heated arguments rarely cause anyone to change his or her mind.

However, if you structure and present an argument well, you can convey your opinion effectively. For example, if you want to go somewhere special with your friends, you may wish to have a later curfew. In order to convince your parents, though, you will want to form an **argument** with responses to any objections they raise. A review of a new movie is another type of argument. Reviewers inform you of their opinion and support the argument with details and examples of why they like or do not like the movie.

In this unit, you will learn how to evaluate arguments presented by people with a variety of viewpoints. You will also learn how to structure your own argument.

Authors have particular **points of view** that they want to express. How they express their points of view, though, depends on their purpose and audience. So you need to ask yourself some questions as you read. What does this author want me to think? Who is the audience for this piece? How does the author try to convince me? Does the argument succeed?

Read the excerpt from *All I Really Need to Know I Learned in Kindergarten* by Robert Fulghum. As you read, put a check in the **Response Notes** by the sentences that tell you the author's opinion.

Response Notes

from **All I Really Need to Know I Learned in Kindergarten** by Robert Fulghum

All I really need to know about how to live and what to do and how to be I learned in kindergarten. Wisdom was not at the top of the graduate-school mountain, but there in the sandpile at Sunday School. These are the things I learned:

Share everything.

Play fair.

Don't hit people.

Put things back where you found them.

Clean up your own mess.

Don't take things that aren't yours.

Say you're sorry when you hurt somebody.

Wash your hands before you eat.

Flush.

Warm cookies and cold milk are good for you.

Live a balanced life—learn some and think some and draw and paint and sing and dance and play and work every day some.

Take a nap every afternoon.

When you go out into the world, watch out for traffic, hold hands, and stick together.

Be aware of wonder. Remember the little seed in the Styrofoam cup: The roots go down and the plant goes up and nobody really knows how or why, but we are all like that.

Goldfish and hamsters and white mice and even the little seed in the Styrofoam cup—they all die. So do we.

And then remember the Dick-and-Jane books and the first word you learned—the biggest word of all—LOOK.

Everything you need to know is in there somewhere. The Golden Rule and love and basic sanitation. Ecology and politics and equality and sane living.

Take any one of those items and extrapolate it into sophisticated adult terms and apply it to your family life or your work or your government or your world and it holds true and clear and firm. Think what a better world it would be if we all—the whole world—had cookies and milk about three o'clock every afternoon and then lay down with our blankies for a nap. Or if all governments had as a basic policy to always put things back where they found them and to clean up their own mess.

And it is still true, no matter how old you are—when you go out into the world, it is best to hold hands and stick together. ❖

✳ Briefly answer the following questions:

■ What is Fulghum's purpose in writing this?

_____

■ Who is his audience?

_____

■ How good is his advice for this audience?

_____

_____

✳ Readers also evaluate an author's argument by how convinced they are. Complete the following statement in a few sentences.

I (am or am not) convinced by Robert Fulghum because

_____

_____

_____

_____

_____

_____

_____

Understanding the author's perspective helps you evaluate his or her opinion.

Support for an argument can come from the author's background or values, as was the case for Robert Fulghum. It can also come from other sources. Expert testimony, facts, and anecdotes—short personal stories that illustrate your point—can all be effective.

"Battle of the Belts" is about the controversy over installing seat belts in school buses. Read the essay to see what the argument is. Mark the **support** Hoffman uses for each side of the "battle" in the **Response Notes.**

Response Notes

"Battle of the Belts" by Karen Epper Hoffman

When Matthew Mandell took his son to meet the school bus that was to take him on a field trip from the Bronx to Lower Manhattan, he was shocked to find the vehicle had no seat belts. Mandell and the other parents protested and ultimately refused to send their kids on the outing. "No child should be in a moving vehicle without a seat belt," he says.

Mandell's surprise is understandable. New York state passed a law in the '80s mandating seat belts on new school buses (although those that predate the law can still be used). Only New York, New Jersey, and Florida require seat belts be installed in new buses; a similar law is going into effect in California in July [2005]. The latest state to join the debate is Illinois—where the state legislature is considering a measure to mandate seat belts on buses.

We can't imagine cars without seat belts; why aren't buses subject to the same regulation? To start with, there's no unanimous agreement they're even necessary. School buses are constructed with high, thickly padded, closely spaced seats that protect passengers by "compartmentalizing" them in a crash, says Charlie Gauthier, executive director of the National Association of State Directors of Pupil Transportation Services. Studies conducted in the late '80s confirmed that compartmentalization works and concluded that seat belts would provide little or no benefit in these vehicles—and may, in some cases, cause injuries.

Consider the figures. Roughly the same number of kids drive or walk to school as take a bus: about 24 million. Yet each year, approximately 169 children are killed being driven to school by an adult, while about a dozen die in school bus crashes. "With or without seat belts, the safest place for a kid to be is on the school bus," Gauthier says.

Plenty of people disagree with Gauthier—the National PTA and the American Academy of Pediatrics support school seat belt laws—and Alan Ross, president of the National Coalition for School Bus Safety, says getting kids in the habit of buckling up every day can save their lives later on.

Seat belts can add $3,000-$6,000 to the cost of a new bus and reduce the number of seats up to 25 percent or more because the newly designed seats take up more room. So districts would have to buy more buses, and pay more mechanics and drivers. These expenses are sticking points in passing legislation that mandates seat belts on buses—or even getting the laws introduced into state legislatures. Lawmakers question whether financially strapped school districts can assume these added costs. Until they can, the kids might just need to hang on tight. ❖

❋ People disagree on the value of seat belts in school buses. The author gives evidence from both sides. Use the graphic organizer to sort the details.

School buses should have seat belts installed.	School buses do not need seat belts.
Evidence: _____	Evidence: _____
Evidence: _____	Evidence: _____
Evidence: _____	Evidence: _____

✳ In each evidence box on page 167, label the type of evidence the author uses.

   E = expert testimony (An expert gives his or her opinion.)

   Fi = figure (A number or percentage is given.)

   A = anecdote (A short story is used to illustrate a point.)

   Fa = fact (The writer uses a statement that can be proven true by consulting a reference source or using firsthand experience.)

   O = opinion (Hoffman tells what she thinks.)

✳ Write a paragraph telling which argument is more convincing to you and why. Include an explanation of how the evidence influenced your answer.

_____

_____

_____

_____

_____

_____

_____

Using different kinds of evidence can make an argument more convincing.

An effective argument is structured around a **main idea** supported by **details** and reasons. Look at the two pieces you read in Lessons 51 and 52. Select one to represent in a cluster in order to show how the details support one of the main ideas. In the large oval, write the main idea of the piece you selected. In the smaller ovals, write supporting details.

Title _____

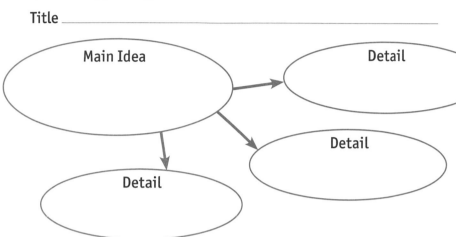

✳ Now use details to support an argument of your own. Select your audience and the opinion you want them to share. The purpose is to convince your audience to share your viewpoint. Create a main idea/details cluster to help you organize your argument. You may want to add more "arms" for more details.

Subject of your argument _____

Opinion _____

Audience _____

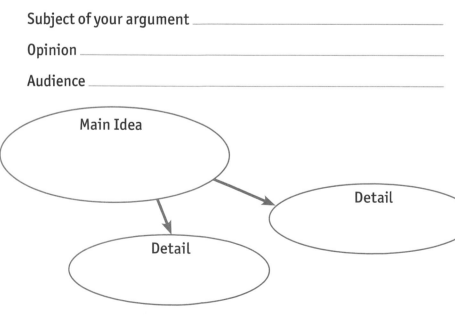

✳ **Write an e-mail presenting your argument in the space below. Begin by clearly stating your main idea. Then build your argument using supporting details. Strengthen your argument by including evidence of different types and from different sources.**

Send

To:

From:

Subject:

Date: Time:

Writers use details and reasons to support the main idea of an argument.

There are at least two sides to every argument. Writers of convincing arguments know that the best way to counter **opposing viewpoints** is to explain how and why the opposing arguments, or counter arguments, are wrong.

As you read this excerpt from *The Greatest: Muhammad Ali* by Walter Dean Myers, ask yourself: What is Myers's viewpoint on the importance of this famous fighter and on prizefighting as a sport? How does Myers handle opposing viewpoints? Circle words or phrases that help you answer these questions.

from **The Greatest: Muhammad Ali** by Walter Dean Myers

Response Notes

In examining the life of Muhammad Ali, his personal and professional choices, and the fighters he faced in the ring, one wonders if it is morally right to allow young men to risk their health and future for the prizes to be found in a fighting career. So many young people have come to the ring from the farms and from the ghettos—Jews, Italians, blacks, Irish, Latinos—all looking for the elusive dreams of fame and fortune. As the fight game grows, and it is growing, perhaps we don't have the right to deny these young people their chance to succeed. But because we know that in so many cases that quest has ended in the physical ruin of lonely warriors who have dropped off the sports pages and out of the public view, we should at least, as Muhammad Ali has done, try to make sure that when people do sacrifice their goods, it is not their only way to secure human dignity.

Courage does not mean letting go of fear. It means having the will to face one's fears, to face the dangers in one's life, and to venture forward to do that which is morally right. Writers have said that Ali was afraid of Liston, that he was afraid of going into the army, that he was afraid of turning away from the Nation of Islam. There were things of which he was afraid, but he was big enough, courageous enough, to face everything that came his way. He has been knocked down in his life, and he has had the courage to rise. ❖

✳ What is your impression of Muhammad Ali from Myers's description?

From the title of his book, you probably think that Myers admires Ali. You are correct. In this selection, he looks at the arguments people have raised against boxing and against Ali, and then he supports the position that we should admire Ali. Use a highlighter to mark the details and arguments that represent Myers's viewpoint. Use a different color to mark the details and arguments of the opposing viewpoint.

✳ In the chart that follows, write Myers's viewpoint at the top of the left column. Write the opposing viewpoint at the top of the right column. Under each heading, write the details from the article that support each viewpoint.

Myers's viewpoint	Opposing viewpoint:
Details:	Details:

✳ Review the e-mail you wrote in Lesson 53. What opposing viewpoint might your audience have? Write an additional paragraph that describes and refutes, or argues against, that argument.

_____

_____

_____

_____

_____

_____

_____

_____

Writers include and argue against opposing viewpoints to strengthen their own arguments.

55 LESSON

When you **evaluate an argument,** you decide whether the argument is convincing. To do that, you need to consider how the author has structured his or her argument.

As you read this excerpt, think about the author's viewpoint and the support for it. Also think about the author's purpose. Circle or underline any strategies he uses, such as using supporting details and facts and arguing against an opposing point of view. Record your observations in the **Response Notes.**

from **Green Planet Rescue** by Robert R. Halpern

Response Notes

"Endangered" sounds like something scary, and it is. "Danger" is right there in the middle of it. But when the subject is endangered plants, it's hard to see what all the fuss is about. Plants just grow, don't they? Weeds sprout in every open space, so what's the problem? There are always plenty of green things out there—everywhere we look. Why is any one plant species all that important?

Plants are not great as pets, but they are our companions on this planet. They are important in our lives and in the lives of every other animal. They produce the basic resources for life on Earth. There may be 380,000 or more different species of plants and we know little about many of them. Some species live in such special and small habitats that we haven't even found them yet. Can we afford to find out what life without a particular species would be like?

An endangered species is one with a small population whose survival is threatened. Human populations are growing. New roads, buildings, dams, farms, and grazing areas are spreading over the landscape so that little real wilderness is left anywhere. An endangered species will disappear if these conditions continue. An endangered species needs help. Today 20,000 to 25,000 of the plant species on Earth are endangered, vulnerable, or rare. We may be losing something important without even knowing much about it. ❖

✳ What is the main point of this article? What is the author's viewpoint in his argument?

✳ Imagine that you are a teacher, and one of your students turned in this article for an assignment on endangered species. On the following form, give it a letter grade based on how well the student supports his or her argument. Remember, you are deciding how effective the argument is, not whether you agree with the writer's viewpoint.

Does the author

- ▪ clearly state his or her main idea?
- ▪ use different kinds of evidence to strengthen the argument?
- ▪ provide details to support the main idea?
- ▪ refute opposing arguments?

Grade assigned for this article: _____

Reasons for this grade: _____

_____

_____

_____

_____

_____

_____

_____

_____

To evaluate an argument, look for how well the details and facts support the author's opinion.

Focusing on Language and Craft

Did you ever think about words having a life of their own? Words come from deep inside us, and they are all around us. It's easy to take them for granted.

Read this short poem by a famous American poet, Emily Dickinson. She wrote these words more than one hundred years ago.

A word is dead when it is said
Some say—
I say it just begins to live
That day—

When we write, we can be careful with our words. We can think about the exact meaning we are trying to convey. We can choose our words so that each word counts. The poems you are going to read in this unit will all be small poems, poems made up of very few words. But each word will be important. In the poems that you write, each word will be important, too.

Have you ever put notes on your refrigerator door with a magnet? Have you found notes that someone in your family has put there for you? There's a story that suggests that William Carlos Williams, a doctor and a poet, put this note on the refrigerator door for his wife.

This Is Just to Say by William Carlos Williams

Response Notes

I have eaten
the plums
that were in
the icebox

and which
you were probably
saving
for breakfast

Forgive me
they were delicious
so sweet
and so cold ❖

* Read the poem again. This time, make notes in the **Response Notes** about what you notice. For example, are there any unusual words? Does the apology sound sincere? Does the missing punctuation make the poem hard to read? How many sentences would there be if it were punctuated like prose?

In this small poem, Williams deals with just one brief moment. It depicts an everyday episode, something that just happened. When Williams wrote the poem, he "magnified" the moment; his "note" captures that moment, and it became a poem that has been read thousands of times.

Most people have an urge to write a poem of their own after reading this one. Try your hand at writing a similar poem.

* Make some notes or draw a picture about a small thing you have done that might require an apology. (You can make it up.)
  - What did you do?
  - Who else was there?
  - What are some words that capture that moment?

* Now, write a poem in the style of Williams's poem. Follow this format:

I have _____

_____

that _____

_____

and which
you _____

_____

for _____

Forgive me
they _____
so _____
and so _____

* Share your poems with others in the class. When you read yours aloud, remember to speak clearly, slowly, and with feeling!

Now, read another short poem by William Carlos Williams. Write your comments in the **Response Notes**.

The Red Wheelbarrow
by William Carlos Williams

so much depends
upon

a red wheel
barrow

glazed with rain
water

beside the white
chickens. ❖

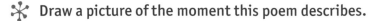

✳ Draw a picture of the moment this poem describes.

✳ With a partner or group, look at your drawing and check for these things:

- Did you draw a red wheelbarrow?
- Did you make it look wet? ("glazed with rain water")
- Do you have white chickens in your drawing?

✳ What else did you put into your drawing?

- Did you give it a background, like a farmyard or backyard in the country?

If you added other details, you were making an inference about the setting. Remember that **making inferences** is one strategy practiced by good readers. Drawing the poem makes use of another important strategy: **visualization.**

This poem could describe a photograph except for the first three words "so much depends." Talk with your partner or group about what you think these words mean.

As a final activity, write a poem on a separate sheet of paper that begins with "so much depends." Make the rest of your poem like a photograph, using only words that describe the picture you have in your mind. Remember, make every word count in this magnified moment.

Magnifying a moment leads to writing that is as vivid as a photograph.

In these next lessons, you are going to read and write a kind of small poem called **haiku.** A haiku is a Japanese poetic form that is very popular worldwide. There are haiku clubs and organizations in the United States in which people write and share haiku. The form is popular because

- ■ it appears to be very simple,
- ■ it features familiar subjects, and
- ■ it invites the reader to give it meaning and significance.

What moment is captured by this haiku, written by the well-known Colorado poet Jim Tipton?

The Sun Coming Up by Jim Tipton

the sun coming up . . .
five eggs
in the iron skillet ✜

Response Notes

✳ With a partner, talk about this poem:
- ■ What colors do you see?
- ■ What kind of skillet is it? What color?
- ■ What can you hear?
- ■ Can you smell the eggs cooking in the skillet?
- ■ Is it cold or warm at dawn?
- ■ Do you feel the warmth of the stove or fire?

✳ Which of these things do you know because the poem actually tells you? Which do you know because you have learned to pay attention to the language and to **make inferences?**
    Put a check beside each question that you could answer because the poem told you. Put a star beside each one that you answered because of an inference you made.

Randy Brooks, a poet, publisher, teacher, and webmaster, has worked with children in schools, introducing them to haiku and leading haiku writing workshops. He writes,

Haiku capture moments of being alive conveyed through sensory images. They do not explain nor describe nor provide philosophical or political commentary. Haiku are gifts of the here and now, deliberately incomplete so that the reader can enter into the haiku moment and experience the feelings of that moment for his or her self.

Haiku are usually made up of two fragments, two images that are placed next to each other. Haiku are not sentences. They are two images unified through an instant in time and a particular place. Sentences are too complete and leave nothing for the imagination of the reader. Haiku are imaginative "jump starts," inviting you to complete the scene that the writer begins. ❖

Many haiku deal with some aspect of nature. Books of haiku are often divided into seasons. Each season is divided into sections such as "birds and beasts," "trees and flowers," "human relationships," and "sky and elements."

With your partner or group, read some of the haiku that sixth graders wrote in Randy's workshop. In the **Response Notes**, jot down images you visualize for each haiku.

Response Notes

Spring

tractor in the field . . .
the doe and her fawn
run from the noise

Summer

good surfing waves . . .
a shark
fin circling

Autumn

hot dogs
sizzling on the grill . . .
smoke up to the moon

Winter

power out . . .
the flickering of the candle
in the kitchen

Working with a partner, reread the explanation of haiku that Randy Brooks wrote. Then look at the students' poems again and notice how well they have learned to write haiku. Talk about which ones you like best and why.

In the next lesson, you will write haiku. Before you leave this lesson, do a Know/Think/Wonder chart about haiku. This chart is different from a K-W-L chart. In this chart, you write what you *know* now, what you *think* but maybe aren't too sure about, and what you still *wonder*—what you'd like to understand better.

KNOW/THINK/WONDER CHART

What I know about haiku now	What I think but am not too sure about	What I wonder, what I'd like to understand better

Haiku pack a lot of meaning into a few words because of the connections and inferences that the reader makes.

You have probably heard the statement "opposites attract." Whether this is true or not, opposites do seem to go together in our language. We contrast *sun and shadow, good and bad, rich and poor, fire and ice.* In preparation for writing your own haiku, it will help to think about opposites.

✳ List some opposites that are common in our language.

Opposites often suggest contrasting images. One pair of opposites is the title of a well-known poem by Robert Frost. Read the poem, making comments in the **Response Notes** about what you notice. What other contrasting ideas and images do you find?

Response Notes

Fire and Ice by Robert Frost

Some say the world will end in fire,
Some say in ice.
From what I've tasted of desire
I hold with those who favor fire.
But if it had to perish twice,
I think I know enough of hate
To say that for destruction ice
Is also great
And would suffice. ✜

✳ What are some ways that "Fire and Ice" is different from the other poems in this unit? How is it the same?

Some things you might have noticed in "Fire and Ice":

- This poem uses a word I don't know: suffice.
- This poem uses rhyme.
- It has punctuation.
- It is about ideas rather than things.
- It is about opposites, how fire or ice might end the world.

✳ You are going to write a haiku using opposite images of animals and plants. Answer the following questions:

What kind of animal are you most like? _____

What kind of plant are you most like? _____

Think about the animal you selected and write the quality that made you select it. It might be a quality like *speedy*, or *graceful*, or *protective*, or *playful*. _____

Do the same thing for the plant. A plant might be *beautiful* like a flower; *strong* like a tree; *prickly* like a rose; *dangerous* like poison ivy or poison oak. _____

Here is a chart filled out by another student. Add your ideas to the chart, using the names of the animal and plant you selected.

Category	Name of animal or plant I am most like	I am most like this animal or plant because of this quality	The opposite of the qualities in Column 2	Name of animal or plant that has the qualities of Column 3
Animal	dolphin	playful	serious	small fish
Plant	oak tree	strong	delicate	blade of grass

Steps in writing your first haiku:

✻ Write a sentence in which the animal in Column 1 does something. Remember the quality you gave it in Column 2.

■ Example: **The dolphin leaps out of the water beside my boat.**

_____

_____

_____

✻ Now write a sentence having the animal in Column 4 do something that contrasts with the sentence above.

■ Example: **The small fish hides in schools in the water, not wanting to be caught.**

_____

_____

_____

Save these sentences for the next lesson when you will write haiku of your own.

Opposite ideas can make powerful images in a poem.

Writing haiku requires close attention to individual words. You must pay attention to **word choice**—finding precisely the right word for what you want to say and making sure each word communicates your thoughts to your readers. Because the traditional haiku uses a set pattern of lines and syllables, you will begin by writing in that form.

Now write your own haiku. Using the sentences you wrote in Lesson 58 as starting points, try to write a poem in the traditional Japanese form of 17 syllables in 3 lines.

✳ Begin by counting the syllables in your sentences.
Example sentences from Lesson 58:

- The dolphin leaps out of the water beside my boat. *(13)*
- The small fish hides in schools in the water. *(10)*

Write your sentences and the number of syllables here:

Sentence 1: _____

_____

Sentence 2: _____

_____

✳ Now think of how the two example sentences are related.

- Dolphins appear to be playful, often following boats and interacting with the people.
- Small fish come up for food, but otherwise hide in groups or schools.

✳ The next step is to try to reduce the number of syllables to 17. Begin by cutting any necessary words. For example, you might say, "the dolphin leaps, water splashes." That would be 8 syllables. Then you could say "small fish disappear under waves." That is 8 syllables. Adding up, you have 16 syllables so you can add one more. If you keep playing with the words, you might end up with something like this:

Example:	dolphins leap, frolic,	5 syllables
	spinning in blue-green waters—	7 syllables
	small fish swim below	5 syllables

This is a traditional haiku in several ways:

- It has three lines of 5, 7, and 5 syllables.
- It has two images or pictures: dolphins and small fish.
- Putting the two images in the same poem requires the reader to think about how they are related.
- As a reader, you might be led to think about the small fish being food for the dolphins, but that is not stated in the poem.

✳ Begin working on your poem. You might want to work with a partner on your first poem, exchanging ideas about how to make your sentences into traditional haiku. Use the checklist below to help you with your writing.

☐ Delete and add whatever words you want. Your finished haiku doesn't have to be tied to the original sentences you wrote. They were just jumping-off points.

☐ Use images of things you can see, smell, taste, touch, or feel.

☐ Use strong verbs. Have your animal do something.

☐ Use adjectives and adverbs to help the reader see your haiku images.

☐ Remember that, in a haiku, every word and syllable must count!

Share your finished haiku with another student. Use this checklist to see whether you need to delete or change any words. Use your own paper for your drafts. Write your finished haiku here:

_____ (title)

_____

_____

_____

by _____ (your name)

Try writing another haiku, this time about the plants you selected. If you'd rather choose another subject, you may, but be sure to make a chart similar to the chart on page 183. That's how you come up with the opposite images that make the haiku!

✳ Write two sentences about the plants with opposite qualities you selected.

Column 1 plant:

_____

_____

_____

Column 4 plant:

_____

_____

_____

✳ Continue writing this haiku in the same way you wrote your first haiku about the animals. Remember to use the checklist on page 186 again.

_____ (title)

_____

_____

_____

by _____ (your name)

Choosing the right words leads to precision and clarity of language.

GREAT SOURCE. COPYING IS PROHIBITED.

One thing to remember about haiku is that they require leaps of imagination. Most haiku use more than one image, as you learned in the last two lessons. The reader must make a leap of imagination to see how the two images can be connected. Different readers will find different ways to make these connections.

One of the greatest writers of the haiku form is Basho. The name Basho (banana tree) is a pseudonym he adopted around 1681 after moving into a hut beside a banana tree. At the time of his death, Basho had 2,000 students, all of whom were eager to learn from the master.

Here are some of Basho's poems. As you read, make notes or sketches around the poems to show what the haiku make you think of and how they make you feel.

Remember: it is the reader who completes the thought of haiku. You need to make the leaps of imagination!

Haiku by Basho

Response Notes

Spring departs
Birds cry
Fishes' eyes are filled with tears ❖

Clouds separate
the two friends—migrating
Wild geese ❖

An old pond!
A frog jumps in—
Splash! in water. ❖

Poverty's child—
starts to grind the rice
and gazes at the moon. ❖

✳ Share your ideas about Basho's poems with a partner or a group.

- Which did you like best? Why?
- Which made use of two images? (Did you draw both images?)
- What connections could you make between the images when there were two of them?

Basho's poems don't seem to be written in the traditional haiku form. We are reading translations. In fact, his poems have been translated by so many people that there are many different versions.

Another Japanese form related to the haiku is the tanka. The tanka starts like the haiku with three lines of 5-7-5 syllables, then adds two more lines of seven syllables each. This gives you a chance to add more details than you can include in three lines. Here are three original tanka written just for the readers of this book. You will see that you can write haiku and tanka about any subject. Read these tanka alone, in pairs, in groups, or as a class. Which form of poem do you prefer?

Use your **Response Notes** to tell what you think and feel about these three tanka.

Three Tanka by Fran Claggett

The girl twirls into
the room, her purple-fringed skirt
making a circle
around her. When she stops, her
moving purple world stands still. ✦

Walking on the beach,
a crow startles me. I watch
its wings form patterns.
Circles and black lines scratch out
letters written on the sand. ✦

The boy hurls the ball.
Crash! goes the window. Inside,
a grown-up boy ducks
from ball and shattering glass.
He throws it back. Yells "Hey!" Grins. ✦

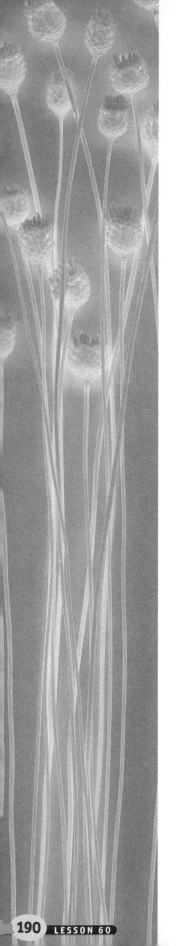

✳ Now you are ready to write more haiku or tanka. They may be traditional or non-traditional. Here are some suggestions for getting started.

- ■ Go for a walk and closely observe the weather, the trees, the wildlife, and outdoor smells and sounds. Make notes in a notebook you keep for this purpose.

- ■ Look at little things through a magnifying glass: the movement of an insect or worm, soil, or a piece of wood.

- ■ Write a haiku structured on two contrasting smells, sounds, or any combination of two sensory impressions.

- ■ See if you get an idea about the contrasts—rising and falling, delicate and firm—but don't try too hard! If the contrast is not based on an observation or experience, your reader won't be able to imagine it.

✳ Use your own notebook for making notes.

✳ Copy your best poem here. You might want to illustrate your poem and share it with the class.

Haiku requires that the writer and reader connect the images with a leap of imagination.

Studying an Author

Reading several works by one author helps you see where stories come from. Gary Paulsen has written more than 130 books of fiction and nonfiction. Most of what he writes comes from his own adventures. Paulsen has landed a plane in an emergency, battled an angry moose, and taken dangerous spills during the Iditarod dogsled race—challenges his fans will recognize in his stories.

One of Paulsen's best-known characters is Brian Robeson, who stars in four books. Gary Paulsen says, "When I set out to write the Brian books I was concerned that everything that happened to Brian should be based on reality, or as near reality as fiction could be. I did not want him to do things that wouldn't or couldn't really happen in his situation. Consequently I decided to write only of things that had happened to me or things I purposely did to make certain they would work for Brian." For example, Paulsen spent several days finding the right rock and then four hours trying to use a hatchet against the rock to light a fire, just for one scene in a book.

An author that serious about his writing deserves further study!

Riding on a sled down a snowy mountain behind a pack of dogs . . . surviving on your own in the wilderness . . . facing an angry bear close up. As Gary Paulsen explores these situations in his books, he uses language and a writing **style** that help the reader feel the excitement, the intensity—and sometimes the danger—of a challenge.

In *Hatchet,* Brian Robeson survives alone in the wilderness for fifty-four days with nothing but a hatchet. In *The River,* Paulsen continues Brian's story. Brian goes back into the wilderness with Derek Holtzer, a psychologist who wants to learn about Brian's survival techniques.

As you read the excerpt from *The River,* pay attention to the words Paulsen uses. In the **Response Notes,** jot down your responses as you read. These can be anything you notice about Paulsen's writing or your opinions about his writing.

from **The River** by Gary Paulsen

Response Notes

He rolled on his side. His body felt stiff, mashed into the ground, and the sudden movement made his vision blur.

There.

He saw Derek—or the form of Derek. He was facedown on his bed, his right hand out, his left arm back and down his side. Blurred, he was all blurred and asleep—how could he be all blurred? Brian shook his head, tried to focus.

Derek was still asleep. How strange, Brian thought—how strange that Derek should still be asleep in the bright daylight, and he knew then that Derek was not sleeping, but did not want to think of the other thing.

Let's reason it out, he thought, his mind as blurred as his vision. Reason it all out. Derek was reaching for the radio and briefcase and the lightning hit the tree next to the shelter and came down the tree and across the air and into Derek and he fell . . .

No.

He was still asleep.

He wasn't that other thing. Not that other word.

But Brian's eyes began to clear then and he saw that Derek was lying with his head to the side and that it was facing Brian and the eyes weren't closed.

They were open.

He was on his side not moving and his eyes were open and Brian thought how strange it was that he would sleep that way—mashed on his stomach.

He knew Derek wasn't sleeping.

He knew.

"No. . . ."

He couldn't be. Couldn't be . . . dead. Not Derek.

Finally, he accepted it.

Brian rose to his hands and knees, stiff and with great slowness, and crawled across the floor of the shelter to where Derek lay.

The large man lay on his stomach as he'd dropped, his head turned to the left. The eyes were not fully open, but partially lidded, and the pupils stared blankly, unfocused toward the back of the shelter.

Brian touched his cheek. He remembered how when the pilot had his heart attack he had felt cool—the dead skin had felt cool.

Derek's skin did not have the coolness, it felt warm; and Brian kneeled next to him and saw that he was breathing.

Tiny little breaths, his chest barely rising and falling, but he was breathing, the air going in and out, and he was not the other word—not dead—and Brian leaned over him.

"Derek?"

There was no answer, no indication that Derek had heard him.

"Derek. Can you hear anything I'm saying?"

Still no sign, no movement. ✣

Look at the notes you took while you read. How do Paulsen's words and writing style make you feel about Brian and the challenges he faces?

_____

_____

_____

_____

_____

_____

_____

_____

_____

_____

✳ Look at the many short sentences and paragraphs Paulsen writes. Listen as you take turns reading the passage aloud with a partner. Paulsen's writing has been called "staccato"—it reads in short "bursts."

Now try using Paulsen's staccato style. Continue Paulsen's story from this point, using words and sentences that continue to build the tension. Some sentences should be short, only 4 to 6 words long.

_____

_____

_____

_____

_____

_____

_____

_____

_____

_____

_____

_____

_____

_____

_____

_____

✳ Read the passage you wrote aloud to a partner. Ask your partner if he or she noted the staccato sentences. Is your partner feeling the tension in your continuation of the story?

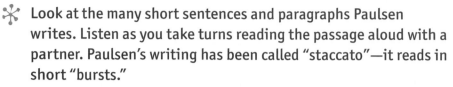

A writer's style can affect the impressions readers get as they read.

The character of Carl in *Dancing Carl* is based on Paulsen's own father. Paulsen's father came home from World War II with both physical and mental scars. In the story, Carl returns many years after the war to the small town where he grew up.

In this excerpt, Marsh (the narrator) and his friend Willy are at the local ice rink. They know that Carl returned from the war with "troubles," and that the town council helped him by giving him a job at the rink and lodging in the warming house. In the warming house, as they get ready to play hockey, Marsh and Willy see Carl act in a surprising way. As you read the excerpt from *Dancing Carl,* write your ideas about what Carl is like in the **Response Notes.**

from **Dancing Carl** by Gary Paulsen

Response Notes

No matter how much you do in the summer, no matter how hard you work or run, your ankles always get weak. The muscles you use for skating don't get used in the summer and it's like everybody has to start all over in the fall, or the first part of winter when the ice forms and gets tight.

The next day was a Friday. School was school. But everybody brought skates and after school we hit the rinks and it was cold and dusky and we went into the warming house to put our skates on.

It was packed. It usually is the first few times after the ice is formed. But this time for some reason there were a lot of little kids, three and four, and like always they were having a rough time.

After skating gets going the warming house isn't so crowded. People skate and come in for a little, then back out, and cycle through that way. But when it first opens they just pack in and the little kids get pushed sideways until they're all in one corner, standing holding their skates, pouting and some of them starting to cry and always before they just had to fight it out or wait until the bigger kids were done and out skating.

But now there was Carl.

He was in the back of the shack and he stood up and he moved into the middle and he took a little girl by the hand and shouldered people out of the way and moved to the benches by the door. There were other kids sitting there, high-school kids suiting up for hockey and he looked at them.

That's all he did. Just looked at them, standing up with his flight jacket unzipped and the little girl holding onto his hand and Willy and I were sitting where we could see his eyes.

"They look hot," he said to me, leaning close to my ear. "His eyes look hot."

And they did. They almost glowed when he looked down at the kids who were sitting on the bench.

For a second or two they didn't do anything, and I think maybe they didn't want to do anything either. But the eyes cut through them, and they moved sideways and some of them got up and they left a place for the little girl and still Carl stood, looking down.

They moved more, made a wider place, and then the people in the center of the room parted and Carl raised his hand and the children who had been pushed down and down came through and they started to use the bench by the door and from that time on whenever the little kids came in they used that part of the bench and nobody else would use that place. Not even the grown-ups who came to skate to the music.

What does Marsh learn about Carl in this scene? Brainstorm a list of character traits—words that describe Carl's personality.

✳ After reading about Carl and the little girl, think about a time when someone acted in a surprising way. Describe what you observed.

✳ Make a list of words that describe the person in your description.

✳ How might the character have changed after the incident you described?

Basing a character on a real person helps a writer create characters that seem vivid and real.

Setting up obstacles, or challenges, for characters is one way a writer creates conflict, an important element of a good story. Writers may use physical conflicts, as in Brian's confrontations with nature. They also use personal or emotional challenges that cause characters to change in important ways.

In this passage from *Dancing Carl,* Marsh brings a model of a World War II B-17 airplane to the rink to show Carl. Through Carl's reaction to the model, Marsh and Willy begin to understand the emotional scars that Carl still carries as the result of the war. As you read the excerpt, write your ideas on why Carl reacts as he does—and why the model affects him so strongly—in the **Response Notes**.

from **Dancing Carl** by Gary Paulsen

Somehow we got to the rink, either with the B-17 flying and carrying me along or with me holding it down, and there wasn't anybody skating.

Not even any kids. So we went in the warming house half figuring it would be closed but Carl was sitting on his bunk. He smiled when we came in, then his face tightened in a quick frown when he saw the plane but I didn't think anything of it.

We knocked snow off and I put the skates and stick in a corner. There was nobody else in the warming house either.

"What's that?" he said, pointing at the stick model.

"It's a model I made. It's a B-17."

"I know that. I know what it is. I mean why do you have it here at the rink?"

"I told him he was crazy . . ." Willy started, laughing.

"Get it out of here."

His voice was quiet, almost like a still pond. Not mad sounding or sad, maybe a little afraid, but so quiet and still that I couldn't quite hear it.

"What?"

"Please take it outside. The model. Please take it out now."

"But it's just a model. If I take it out the wind will tear it apart." Like I said, I had a lot of work in it. I'd probably ruin it later, the way you do with models. Maybe put lighter fluid on the tail and send her off a roof. But that was later, now it was still a fresh model and I hated to just throw it out in the snow and let the wind tear it apart. "I'll put it over in the corner."

"Did you have something to do with B-17's during the war?" Willy asked and it was something he shouldn't have asked, not then, not ever.

Carl turned from the plane to Willy and there was a hunted look in his eyes. No, more than that, more a torn thing, a broken thing—as if something inside had ripped and torn loose and left him broken and he looked at the model and his face wrinkled down and I knew it wasn't a model anymore, knew he wasn't in the warming house.

"Colors," he said, whispering. "Colors red and down and going around and around in tighter and tighter circles. Hot. Colors hot and alive and going down."

Willy stepped back. "I'm sorry. I didn't mean to say anything ..."

But it was done. His whisper changed to a hiss, hot and alive, and he stood in the warming house and got into the open place by the door. I dumped the model in a corner, dumped it without looking, and moved away.

Carl stood with his arms out, still making that hissing sound, and I wondered if I could get out of the warming house and go for help, get the police, but he was by the door and I was afraid to go past him. Not afraid that he'd do something to me, afraid that I'd hurt him somehow.

So I stood, we stood, and Carl moved his arms even tighter out and the hiss changed to a kind of growl and I realized that he was a plane, a large plane, and I could see it wheeling through the sky, engines rumbling and I knew then that it was a B-17.

Through two, then three loops around the open area in the warming house Carl moved, turning and banking slowly and I swear you could see the plane.

Then something happened. Something hit or hurt the plane, one arm, one wing folded up and over and the plane went down, circling in a great spiral as it went down.

I mean Carl. Carl went down. But it was a plane, too. There in the warming house there was something that Carl did that made him seem a great bomber with a broken wing going down, around and down and I could see it. See the smoke and the explosion as the shell took the wing, the way I'd seen it in newsreels, and then the plane coming down, all the lines coming down, down to the ground in a crash that was like a plane and like a bird, too. ❖

✳ Marsh describes Carl as "torn" and "broken." What does he mean by this?

_____

_____

_____

_____

_____

✳ Use the chart below to explore how Carl's experiences in World War II changed him. The first excerpt from *Dancing Carl* in Lesson 62 gives us a glimpse of what Carl might have been like before the war. Use the character traits you brainstormed on page 196 to help you describe what kind of person Carl might have been. Then use the second excerpt to describe what Carl is like as a result of the war.

Before the War	After the War
Carl may have lacked compassion.	Carl protects those who can't stand up for themselves.

> When you read about a character confronting a challenge, try to figure out how and why the experience changes the character.

In many of Paulsen's books, the main characters deal with the challenges of nature—hunger, cold, the fear of being lost. Paulsen not only depicts the struggles characters face, but he also explores what the characters need to do and think in order to survive the challenges.

Dogsong is not a true story, but it is based on Paulsen's experiences with dog-sledding. The main character, Russel Susskit, is a fourteen-year-old Eskimo boy. Russel becomes friends with Oogruk, an old man who teaches him about dogs, sledding, nature, and the "Old Ways." Russel then goes on a journey of his own, where he meets with many challenges at the hands of nature.

As you read from *Dogsong* (which Paulsen has called his favorite book), put an "X" in the **Response Notes** near any parts that focus on challenges in nature.

from Dogsong by Gary Paulsen

Response Notes

When the first dog started to weave with exhaustion, still pulling, but slipping back and forth as it pulled, he sensed their tiredness in the black night and stopped the team. He had a piece of meat in the sled, deer meat from a leg and he cut it in six pieces. When he'd pulled them under an overhanging ledge out of the wind and tipped the sled on its side, he fed them. But they were too tired to eat and slept with the meat between their legs.

He didn't know that they could become that tired and the knowledge frightened him. He was north, in the open, and the dogs wouldn't eat and they were over a hundred and fifty miles to anything. Without the dogs, he would die.

Without the dogs he was nothing.

He'd never felt so alone and for a time fear roared in him. The darkness became an enemy, the cold a killer, the night a ghost from the underworld that would take him down where demons would tear strips off him.

He tried a bite of the meat but he wasn't hungry. Not from tiredness. At least he didn't think so.

But he knew he wasn't thinking too well, and so he lay down between the two wheel-dogs and pulled them close on either side and took a kind of sleep.

Brain-rest more than sleep. He closed his eyes and something inside him rested. The darkness came harder and the northern lights danced and he rested. He was not sure how long it might have been, but it was still dark when one of the dogs got up and moved in a circle to find a better resting position.

The dog awakened the remainder of the team and they all ate their meat with quiet growls of satisfaction that came from their stomachs up through their throats. Small rumbles that could be felt more than heard.

When they'd eaten they lay down again, not even pausing to relieve themselves. And Russel let them stay down for all of that long night. He dozed now with his eyes open, still between the two wheel-dogs, until the light came briefly.

Then he stood and stretched, feeling the stiffness. The dogs didn't get up and he had to go up the line and lift them. They shook hard to loosen their muscles and drop the tightness of sleeping long.

"Up now! Up and out."

Out.

They started north again, into a land that Russel did not know. At first the dogs ran poorly, raggedly, hating it. But inside half a mile they had settled into their stride and were a working team once more.

But they had lost weight.

In the long run they had lost much weight and it was necessary for Russel to make meat. He didn't know how long they could go without meat but he didn't think it could be long.

He had to hunt.

If he did not get meat the dogs would go down—and he was nothing without the dogs. He had to get food for them.

The light ended the dark-fears but did not bring much warmth. Only the top edge of the sun slipped into view above the horizon, so there was no heat from it.

To get his body warm again after the long night of being still he held onto the sled and ran between the runners. He would run until his breath grew short, then jump on and catch his wind, then run again. It took a few miles of that to get him warm and as soon as he was, the great hole of hunger opened in his stomach and he nearly fell off the sled. ❖

❋ "Without the dogs he was nothing." What do you think Paulsen means by these words?

_____

_____

_____

_____

_____

✳ Choose four challenges in nature that Russel encounters. Put them in order from 1 (the most crucial, or life-threatening) to 4 (the least crucial). After each challenge, explain why you ranked the challenge as you did. (For example, "It's important to have enough food, but if Russel doesn't stay warm, he won't be able to hunt.") Compare your chart with others in a small group.

Challenge 1

Challenge 2

Challenge 3

Challenge 4

Reading about characters confronting challenges in nature gives us a glimpse of how people act and think when tested by extreme conditions.

Gary Paulsen has based fictional stories on real people and real experiences, but he has also written about his own experiences. In *Woodsong,* an **autobiography,** he talks about his sled dogs and competing in the Iditarod, a grueling dogsled race across Alaska.

In this selection, Paulsen is describing a time when he burns left-over food to dispose of it—and the smell attracts a big, hungry bear that Paulsen calls "Scarhead." As you read the excerpt, think about what Paulsen is learning from the experience. Write down your ideas in the **Response Notes.**

Response Notes

from **Woodsong** by Gary Paulsen

He was having a grand time. The fire didn't bother him. He was trying to reach a paw in around the edges of flame to get at whatever smelled so good. He had torn things apart quite a bit—ripped one side off the burn enclosure—and I was having a bad day and it made me mad.

I was standing across the burning fire from him and without thinking—because I was so used to him—I picked up a stick, threw it at him, and yelled, "Get out of here."

I have made many mistakes in my life, and will probably make many more, but I hope never to throw a stick at a bear again.

In one rolling motion—the muscles seemed to move within the skin so fast that I couldn't take half a breath—he turned and came for me. Close. I could smell his breath and see the red around the sides of his eyes. Close on me he stopped and raised on his back legs and hung over me, his forelegs and paws hanging down, weaving back and forth gently as he took his time and decided whether or not to tear my head off.

I could not move, would not have time to react. I knew I had nothing to say about it. One blow would break my neck. Whether I lived or died depended on him, on his thinking, on his ideas about me—whether I was worth the bother or not.

I did not think then.

Looking back on it I don't remember having one coherent thought when it was happening. All I knew was terrible menace. His eyes looked very small as he studied me. He looked down on me for what seemed hours. I did not move, did not breathe, did not think or do anything.

And he lowered.

Perhaps I was not worth the trouble. He lowered slowly and turned back to the trash and I walked backward halfway to the house and then ran—anger growing now—and took the rifle from the gun rack by the door and came back out.

He was still there, rummaging through the trash. I worked the bolt and fed a cartridge in and aimed at the place where you kill bears and began to squeeze. In raw anger, I began to take up the four pounds of pull necessary to send death into him.

And stopped.

Kill him for what?

That thought crept in.

Kill him for what?

For not killing me? For letting me know it is wrong to throw sticks at four-hundred-pound bears? For not hurting me, for not killing me, I should kill him? I lowered the rifle and ejected the shell and put the gun away. I hope Scarhead is still alive. For what he taught me, I hope he lives long and is very happy because I learned then—looking up at him while he made up his mind whether or not to end me—that when it is all boiled down I am nothing more and nothing less than any other animal in the woods. ❖

❊ Compare Paulsen's experience with the bear to a challenge faced by one of the characters in his novels. Think about the characters you've read about in this unit or use your knowledge of other books by Gary Paulsen. Record your ideas in the chart.

Paulsen's challenge	How Paulsen changed

Character's challenge	How character changed

※ Think about a challenging experience that you have faced. Write notes for an excerpt from your autobiography. Describe the experience, what you learned from it, and how it changed you.

The experience

What I learned from it

How it changed me

Writers share events from their lives not only to tell what happened, but also to tell what makes those events important.

Assessing Your Repertoire

The goal of this *Daybook* has been to help you become a more confident reader and writer. As you read and write on your own, you won't need to think through every strategy each time you open a book or get ready to write. You have gained confidence, just like an experienced rock climber or skateboarder. And just like an experienced athlete, you will become even more confident over time.

In the *Daybook*, you have practiced strategies and skills that build reading and writing confidence, and you stopped to measure your progress. In this last unit, you will read two short stories by award-winning author Sandra Cisneros. You will use the skills and strategies you have practiced throughout this book and will check to see how well you have learned them.

66 STUDYING AN AUTHOR

Sandra Cisneros, author of the two stories you are going to read, is the daughter of a Mexican father and a Mexican American mother. She was the only girl in a family of seven children. Her family moved between Chicago, where she was born, and Mexico, where her father had many relatives. Her stories often reflect her life in both places.

Cisneros writes, ". . . I currently earn my living by my pen. I live in San Antonio, Texas, in a violet house filled with many creatures, little and large." Pictures of her often show her with four dogs!

Her first book to attract attention and receive many awards was *The House on Mango Street*. This is the story of Esperanza Cordero, a young girl growing up in the Hispanic quarter of Chicago. The story is told in a series of small journal entries, the kind you might write in your own journal or diary. Together, they reflect the ups and downs of the everyday life of Esperanza. They show her in moments of sadness and moments of joy. If you read the whole book, you get a rich picture of all the dimensions of one young girl. The story in the next lesson called "My Name" is from this book.

You will also read one of Sandra Cisneros's best-known stories, "Eleven," which is from her book, *Woman Hollering Creek and Other Stories*. It has also received many awards.

INTERACT WITH THE TEXT
Read the story "Eleven," using the **Response Notes** to predict, question, connect, or visualize as you read.

"Eleven" from *Woman Hollering Creek and Other Stories* by Sandra Cisneros

Response Notes

What they don't understand about birthdays and what they never tell you is that when you're eleven, you're also ten, and nine, and eight, and seven, and six, and five, and four, and three, and two, and one. And when you wake up on your eleventh birthday you expect to feel eleven, but you don't. You open your eyes and everything's just like yesterday, only it's today. And you don't feel eleven at all. You feel like you're still ten. And you are—underneath the year that makes you eleven.

Like some days you might say something stupid, and that's the part of you that's still ten. Or maybe some days you might need to sit on your mama's lap because you're scared, and that's the part of you that's five. And maybe one day when you're all grown up maybe you will need to cry like if you're three, and that's okay. That's what I tell Mama when she's sad and needs to cry. Maybe she's feeling three.

Because the way you grow old is kind of like an onion or like the rings inside a tree trunk or like my little wooden dolls that fit one inside the other, each year inside the next one. That's how being eleven years old is.

You don't feel eleven. Not right away. It takes a few days, weeks even, sometimes even months before you say Eleven when they ask you. And you don't feel smart eleven, not until you're almost twelve. That's the way it is.

Only today I wish I didn't have only eleven years rattling inside me like pennies in a tin Band-Aid box. Today I wish I was one hundred and two instead of eleven because if I was one hundred and two I'd have known what to say when Mrs. Price put the red sweater on my desk. I would've known how to tell her it wasn't mine instead of just sitting there with that look on my face and nothing coming out of my mouth.

"Whose is this?" Mrs. Price says, and she holds the red sweater up in the air for all the class to see. "Whose? It's been sitting in the coatroom for a month."

"Not mine," says everybody. "Not me."

"It has to belong to somebody," Mrs. Price keeps saying, but nobody can remember. It's an ugly sweater with red plastic buttons and a collar and sleeves all stretched out like you could use it for a jump rope. It's maybe a thousand years old and even if it belonged to me I wouldn't say so.

Maybe because I'm skinny, maybe because she doesn't like me, that stupid Sylvia Saldivar says, "I think it belongs to Rachel." An ugly sweater like that, all raggedy and old, but Mrs. Price believes her. Mrs. Price takes the sweater and puts it right on my desk, but when I open my mouth nothing comes out.

"That's not, I don't, you're not...Not mine," I finally say in a little voice that was maybe me when I was four.

"Of course it's yours," Mrs. Price says. "I remember you wearing it once." Because she's older and the teacher, she's right and I'm not.

Not mine, not mine, not mine, but Mrs. Price is already turning to page thirty-two, and math problem number four. I don't know why but all of a sudden I'm feeling sick inside, like the part of me that's three wants to come out of my eyes, only I squeeze them shut tight and bite down on my teeth real hard and try to remember today I am eleven, eleven. Mama is making a cake for me tonight and when Papa comes home everybody will sing Happy birthday, happy birthday to you.

But when the sick feeling goes away and I open my eyes, the red sweater's still sitting there like a big red mountain. I move the red sweater to the corner of my desk with my ruler. I move my pencil and books and eraser as far from it as possible. I even move my chair a little to the right. Not mine, not mine, not mine.

In my head I'm thinking how long till lunchtime, how long till I can take the red sweater and throw it over the schoolyard fence, or leave it hanging on a parking meter, or bunch it up into a little ball and toss it in the alley. Except when math period ends Mrs. Price says loud and in front of everybody, "Now, Rachel, that's enough," because she sees I've shoved the red sweater to the tippy-tip corner of my desk and it's hanging all over the edge like a waterfall, but I don't care.

"Rachel," Mrs. Price says. She says it like she's getting mad. "You put that sweater on right now and no more nonsense."

"But it's not—"

"Now!" Mrs. Price says.

This is when I wish I wasn't eleven, because all the years inside of me—ten, nine, eight, seven, six, five, four, three, two, and one—are pushing at the back of my eyes when I put one arm through one sleeve of the sweater that smells like cottage cheese, and then the other arm through the other and stand there with my arms apart like if the sweater hurts me and it does, all itchy and full of germs that aren't even mine.

That's when everything I've been holding in since this morning, since when Mrs. Price put the sweater on my desk, finally lets go, and all of a sudden I'm crying in front of everybody. I wish I was invisible but I'm not. I'm eleven and it's my birthday today and I'm crying like I'm three in front of everybody. I put my head down on the desk and bury my face in my stupid clown-sweater arms. My face all hot and spit coming out of my mouth because I can't stop the little animal noises from coming out of me, until there aren't any more tears left in my eyes, and it's just my body shaking like when you have the hiccups, and my whole head hurts like when you drink milk too fast.

But the worst part is right before the bell rings for lunch. That stupid Phyllis Lopez, who is even dumber than Sylvia Saldivar, says she remembers the red sweater is hers! I take it off right away and give it to her, only Mrs.Price pretends like everything's okay.

Today I'm eleven. There's a cake Mama's making for tonight, and when Papa comes home from work we'll eat it. There'll be candles and presents and everybody will sing Happy birthday, happy birthday to you, Rachel, only it's too late.

I'm eleven today. I'm eleven, ten, nine, eight, seven, six, five, four, three, two, and one, but I wish I was one hundred and two. I wish I was anything but eleven, because I want today to be far away already, far away like a runaway balloon, like a tiny *o* in the sky, so tiny-tiny you have to close your eyes to see it. ❖

Response Notes

VISUALIZE

✳ Draw a picture of how you think Rachel feels when she is sitting in her classroom with the ugly red sweater. In the space below, write how you feel about Rachel's reaction to the sweater.

_____

_____

_____

_____

MAKE CONNECTIONS

Think of times when you didn't feel as old as you were.

✳ Make notes about one memory you have when you felt younger than you were.

■ What made you feel younger?

■ How old were you?

■ How old did you feel?

✳ Jot down as many details as you can remember about that memory. You will use these notes in a later lesson.

_____

_____

_____

_____

_____

_____

✳ Write a sentence about whether you think boys and girls both have experiences like Rachel's, when they don't feel as old as they are.

_____

_____

Responding to the emotions of the characters in a story helps the reader get more meaning from it.

One of the ways to read a piece of literature is to think "what if?" the story were different in some way. For example, how would your **perspective,** or point of view, change if the title or a character changed?

✳ Talk with a partner about how you might read this story differently if the title were different.

■ What other title would fit this piece? Would another title be more or less effective than "Eleven"? Write your thoughts.

_____

_____

_____

_____

✳ Talk with a partner about how the story would change if it were told from a different perspective.

■ What if "Eleven" were a story of a boy at that age instead of a girl? How do you think the story would be different?

■ What if you were a student in Rachel's class who remembered this moment of insensitivity toward Rachel? How do you think you would feel about this story now?

_____

_____

_____

_____

_____

✳ Make up three or four additional "what if" speculations and share them with your partner or writing group.

_____

_____

_____

_____

✳ Choose one of the "what if" speculations. Make some planning notes about details you could include when you write about this speculation. Save these notes.

Speculating leads to new ways of making meaning from a story or poem.

Read the story "My Name" from *The House on Mango Street* by Sandra Cisneros, using the **Response Notes** to mark any places where you are aware of the influence of the Spanish language. You may want to make other comments about your reactions as you read, too.

"My Name" from *The House on Mango Street*
by Sandra Cisneros

Response Notes

In English my name means hope. In Spanish it means too many letters. It means sadness, it means waiting. It is like the number nine. A muddy color. It is the Mexican records my father plays on Sunday mornings when he is shaving, songs like sobbing.

It was my great-grandmother's name and now it is mine. She was a horse-woman too, born like me in the Chinese year of the horse—which is supposed to be bad luck if you're born female—but I think this is a Chinese lie because Chinese, like Mexicans, don't like their women strong.

My great-grandmother. I would've liked to have known her, a wild horse of a woman, so wild she wouldn't marry. Until my great-grandfather threw a sack over her head and carried her off. Just like that, as if she were a fancy chandelier. That's the way he did it.

And the story goes she never forgave him. She looked out the window her whole life, the way so many women sit their sadness on an elbow. I wonder if she made the best with what she got or was she sorry because she couldn't be all the things she wanted to be. Esperanza. I have inherited her name, but I don't want to inherit her place by the window.

At school they say my name funny as if the syllables were made out of tin and hurt the roof of your mouth. But in Spanish my name is made out of softer something like silver, not quite as thick as sister's name—Magdalena—which is uglier than mine. Magdalena who at least can come home and become Nenny. But I am always Esperanza.

I would like to baptize myself under a new name, a name more like the real me, the one nobody sees. Esperanza as Lisandra or Maritza or Zeze the X. Yes. Something like Zeze the X will do. ❖

Cisneros uses language in poetic ways.

❋ What do you think Esperanza means when she says " . . . in Span-ish my name is made out of softer something like silver"?

_____

_____

❋ Write your name. Then write what you think your name could be "made out of."

_____

_____

❋ What do you visualize when you read the phrase "the way so many women sit their sadness on an elbow"?

_____

_____

❋ Find another example of a poetic use of language in "My Name."

_____

_____

What if you had a different name? Would it affect who you are?

❋ Jot down names that you may have tried at different times in your life.

_____

_____

❋ Think about whether you would act differently if you had another name.

_____

_____

❋ Do different people call you by different names? Make notes about any of these names and how you feel about them.

_____

_____

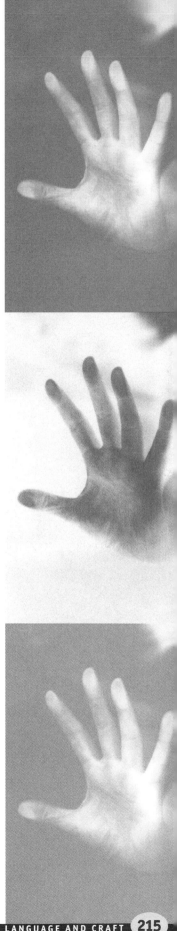

✳ If you use a nickname, make notes about how the nickname affects you and the way others respond to you.

✳ Many writers and actors use a pseudonym, which means "false name." Think of a pseudonym for yourself. Jot that name down along with a note about why you chose it.

✳ Choose one of the questions above and make a cluster about your ideas. Here are some suggestions for your cluster.

  ■ Explain what your name means to different people you know.

  ■ Describe ideas about how you got your nickname or why you chose your pseudonym.

✳ Put your name in the middle of an oval. Then make a cluster using as many details as you can remember for one of these ideas. Include things like place, dialogue, action, feelings, and any sensory details you can think of—taste, sound, and so on. Share your cluster with a partner or a writing group. Save it to use in a later lesson.

My Name or Pseudonym

Reflecting on the importance of names leads to a deeper understanding of a text and the characters.

In this lesson you will review the work you did in Lessons 66-68. This will prepare you to write a piece that shows what you have learned about how authors get messages across to their readers.

Here are the notes you should have from your work:

1 **A memory:** notes about one memory of a time when you didn't feel as old as you were (from Lesson 66)

2 **Other ways you might read "Eleven":** speculations on ways you might read the story "Eleven" differently (from Lesson 67)

3 **Poetic language** from "My Name" (from Lesson 68)

4 **How your name has been important to you:** notes about your name—other names people call you, nicknames, names you wish you had, how your name has been important (from Lesson 68)

✳ Review your notes. Choose one topic to develop into a personal essay. Write the topic you have selected here.

_____

_____

Using the notes you have as a starting point, make additional notes.

✳ If you have chosen to write about an incident, an event that happened, be sure to include such details as

- ■ time and place
- ■ what actually happened
- ■ who was there
- ■ what people there said
- ■ how it ended

Tell how you felt about the incident at the time and how you feel about it now.

_____

_____

_____

_____

✳ If you have chosen to write about another way to read the story, be sure to include the following.

- ■ what you think should be changed
- ■ why you think your ideas would improve the story
- ■ how your changes would affect the characters

Use these writing lines to plan your writing.

_____

_____

_____

_____

_____

_____

_____

_____

_____

_____

_____

_____

_____

_____

_____

_____

_____

_____

You are now ready to write a draft of your paper. Use your notes, and write at least a page on regular notebook paper. Use details so that your audience has a clear picture of your story or your ideas.

Using notes, drawings, and other prewriting material helps in writing organized and detailed papers.

As with any craft, one very important part of writing is looking to see how it can be improved. This is called *revision* because you *see (vision)* it *again (re-)*. Work with a partner to decide how you can improve your writing. Ask each other questions such as the ones below. Then, use the list to help you evaluate your own writing.

- Does the beginning get your attention so you want to read more? If not, how could it be improved?

- Do I stay on topic? If not, where do I get off topic?

- Do I use "vivid verbs" to show action? Where are some places where I could use stronger verbs?

- Do I use specific, concrete details and sensory language to make my piece come alive? Where could I use more details?

- Is the ending satisfying? Does it sound "finished"? If not, what could I do to make a better ending?

- Are my sentences complete? Do I use a variety of sentences? If not, where do I need to make changes?

- Have I checked for any spelling or punctuation errors? If not, do it now!

Characteristics of my paper	Really good!	So-so (about average)	Needs improve-ment!
Does it have a catchy beginning?			
Does it stay on topic?			
Does it use vivid verbs?			
Does it use details and sensory language effectively?			
Does it have a good ending?			
Does it use complete sentences?			
Are the words spelled correctly?			

After you have made the changes that you think will strengthen your writing, make a final copy.

A FINAL REFLECTION

As you worked through this book, you had many opportunities to learn and practice skills and strategies to become a better reader and writer. You have read stories, poems, and essays, using these skills and strategies.

In this final reflection, identify one strategy you have perfected during your work with the *Daybook*. Think about whether you have met the goal: that you now *like* to read and write. Then write a note to a friend that explains how your work with the *Daybook* has helped you become a better reader and writer.

Using a list of traits of good writing makes self-assessment easier.

Becoming An Active Reader

Reading can entertain, inform, and reward. Reading also requires some hard work on the part of the reader. The sections that follow will help you get the most out of your reading.

The **reading process** section will guide you through reading a text. It will help you think about how to prepare to read (before reading), what to think about as you read (during reading), and how to get the most out of your reading by reflecting on it (after reading).

The **reading actively** section will show you how to interact with a text in order to get the most meaning out of it. It will show you how to engage with a text by using your brain and your pen—both at the same time!

The Reading Process has three parts: **Before Reading, During Reading,** and **After Reading.**

1. BEFORE READING

✳ Preview the Material

Look over the selection before you read. Does the selection look like a short story or other work of fiction? If so, look at the title, introduction, and illustrations. Does the selection look like nonfiction? If so, look for headings, boldfaced words, photos, and captions. Also, ask yourself how the information is organized. Is the author comparing or contrasting information about the topic? Is the information presented in a sequence using signal words like first, second, third, and finally? Understanding how an author has organized information will help you to recognize key points as you read.

✳ Make Predictions

When you make predictions, you actively connect with the words on the page. Think about what you already know about the subject or the images. Then, think of yourself as a text detective, putting together what you know with new details in the text. Predict what you think will happen, why an event caused something to happen, or what might come next in a series of events.

✳ Set a Purpose

Begin by reviewing what you already know about the topic or situation in the text. Then, think about what you want to find out.

QUESTIONS TO ASK YOURSELF BEFORE READING

- ■ Before I read this material, what do I think it is going to be about?
- ■ After looking over the selection, what do I already know about this subject?
- ■ What should I be thinking about as I read?

2. DURING READING

✳ Engage with the Text

As your eyes look at the words, your brain should be working to make connections between the words and what you already know. Have you had an experience similar to that of one of the characters in a story you are reading? Do you know someone like the character? Have you read another book about the topic? You will also want to connect what you read to the predictions you made before reading. *Confirm, revise, predict again* is a cycle that continues until you finish reading the material. All of these questions will go on inside your head. Sometimes, though, it helps to think out loud or write.

✳ Monitor Your Understanding

As you read, stop from time to time and ask yourself, "Do I understand what I just read?" If the text doesn't make sense, there are several steps that you can take.

- Go back and reread the text carefully.
- Read on to see if more information helps you understand.
- Pull together the author's ideas in a summary.
- Retell, or say in your own words, the events that have happened.
- Picture in your mind what the author described.
- Look for context clues or word-structure clues to help you figure out hard words.

This takes some practice. Remember, to be a successful reader, you must be an active reader. Make an effort to check your understanding every so often when you read a new selection.

QUESTIONS TO ASK YOURSELF WHILE YOU ARE READING

- What important details am I finding?
- Which of these ideas seem to be the most important?
- Does this information fit with anything I already know?
- What do I see in my mind as I read this material?
- Do I understand the information in the charts or tables? Does it help me to understand what I am reading?

3. AFTER READING

✳ Summarize
Reread to locate the most important ideas in the story or essay.

✳ Respond and Reflect
Talk with a partner about what you have read. What did you learn from the text? Were your predictions confirmed? What questions do you still have? Talking about reading helps you to better understand what you have read.

✳ Ask Questions
Try asking yourself questions that begin like this:

*Can I compare or contrast . . . evaluate . . . connect . . .
examine . . . analyze . . . relate . . .*

✳ Engage with the Text
Good readers engage with a text all the time, even when they have finished reading. When you tie events in your life or something else you have read to what you are currently reading or have read, you become more involved with your reading. In the process, you are learning more about your values, relationships in your family, and issues in the world around you.

QUESTIONS TO ASK YOURSELF AFTER READING

- ■ What was this article about?
- ■ What was the author trying to tell me?
- ■ Have I learned something that made me change the way I think about this topic?
- ■ Are there parts of this material that I really want to remember?

Make the effort to stay involved with your reading by reading actively. Your mind should be busy reading the text, making connections, making predictions, and asking questions. Your hand should be busy, too. Keep track of what you are thinking by "reading with your pen." **Write** your reactions to the text or connections that you can make. **Circle** words you don't understand. **Draw** a sketch of a scene. **Underline** or **highlight** an important idea. You may have your own way of reading actively. You may develop a style that works better for you, but here are six common ways of reading actively.

MARK OR HIGHLIGHT The most common way of noting important parts of a text is to write on a sticky note and put it on the page. Or, if you can, mark important parts of a text by highlighting them with a marker, pen, or pencil. You can also use highlighting tape. The highlighted parts should provide a good review of the text.

ASK QUESTIONS Asking questions is a way of engaging the author in conversation. Readers who ask a lot of questions think about the text more and understand it better. "Why is the writer talking about this?" "Is this really true?" "What does that mean?"

REACT AND CONNECT When you read, listen to the author and to yourself. Think about what you are reading and relate it to your own life. Compare and contrast what the text says to what you know.

PREDICT Readers who are involved with the text constantly wonder how things will turn out. They think about what might happen. They check their thoughts against the text and make adjustments. Sometimes the author surprises them! Making predictions helps you stay interested in what you are reading.

VISUALIZE Making pictures in your mind can help you "see"what you are thinking and help you remember. A chart, a sketch, a diagram— any of these can help you "see." Sometimes your picture doesn't match what you think the author is telling you. This is a signal to reread to check your understanding of the text.

CLARIFY As you read, you need to be sure that you understand what is going on in the text. Take time to pull together what you have learned. Try writing notes to clarify your understanding. Another way of checking to see that you understand is to tell someone about what you have read.

GLOSSARY

aggressor a person or country that attacks another

apparatus equipment for a specific purpose

architect a person who designs buildings or other large structures

arcing [AR king] moving in a curved path

argument persuasive language consisting of a main idea supported by details and reasons

associate be with; play with

author's purpose the reason an author writes a specific piece

autobiography an author's story of his or her own life

B-17 a bomber plane used in World War II; also known as the "Flying Fortress"

banking tilting sideways when making a turn

bar graph a graph in which bars represent data values

barrio [BAR ee oh] a Spanish-speaking area of a city

benevolent showing kindness or generosity

bickering spiteful arguing and quarreling

binoculars a device made up of two small telescopes that are attached in the middle. You can look through this device with both eyes to make distant things look bigger.

Black student movement a group of African American college students who fought for equal rights during the 1960s

bloomers loose-fitting women's underwear

blurred out of focus, unclear

bonds something, like rope, that is used to restrain

bow the front part of a ship

bulkhead a separate section of a ship or plane

burial chamber a room that serves as a tomb

cadence rhythmic sound of speech

caravan a trailer; a large truck with furniture in it that can be used as a home

causes and effects the ways in which events (causes) bring on other events (effects)

characterization the way an author develops the people, animals, and imaginary creatures in a story

climax the highest point, or turning point, in the action of a story

coherent consistent within itself; logical

communal shared by many people

compartment a separate space or room

compartmentalize to separate into different areas

compounded increased by combining

concussion damage due to a hard blow

con permiso [cohn pair MEE soh] excuse me

conveyor belt a continuously moving belt used to transport materials from one place to another

crane a long-legged, long-necked bird that wades in marshes and wetlands and soars over open areas

creaky raspy; having a grating or squeaky sound

credible believable

critical reading a reading strategy that involves understanding and evaluating information outside a text

crow's nest a small lookout platform that is near the top of a ship's mast

deafening so loud as to cause hearing loss

dehydrating causing a lack of moisture

denounce to publicly speak out against

description a basic technique an author uses to create pictures in the mind of a reader

devoured eaten up

diagram an illustration that shows the parts of something or how it works

disabled impaired; not able to function properly

disposition usual mood or temperament

distress confused anxiety

drenched soaking wet

dungeon an ancient prison often found in a castle basement

dusky dim; shadowy; nearing sunset

eccentric strange; odd

ecstatic extremely happy; joyful

Egyptologist person who studies artifacts of ancient Egypt

elicit to bring forth

el Polo Norte [el POH loh NOR tay] the North Pole

engineer someone who designs or plans things

evaluate an argument to decide whether an argument is convincing

excruciating intensely painful; agonizing

existence life

exposition the part of the story, usually the beginning, that explains the background and setting and introduces the characters

extrapolate to predict a future situation by drawing on similar situations in the present or past

falling action the part of a story that follows the climax; it contains the action or dialogue necessary to lead the story to a resolution or ending

figurative language a way that poets convey more images with fewer words; techniques include metaphor and simile

filling station gas station

flight jacket a style of leather jacket worn by airplane pilots; sometimes called a "bomber jacket"

flirting behaving in a tempting way

foibles small weaknesses or mistakes

forage to search for food

forensic referring to the use of science or technology to find facts or evidence

fowls domesticated birds that are used for food, such as chickens, ducks, and turkeys

frantically in a hurried and disorganized manner

fretted worried

full steam without any hesitation

game wild animals, fish, and birds hunted for food

gangsters criminals; outlaws

glint a sparkle; a flash of light

go down to die: an animal handler's expression

gratitude thankfulness, appreciation

grindstone a large stone that is used to sharpen or polish knives and tools

gruesome horrifying, disgusting; repulsive

guileless not deceitful

guillotine (GHEE oh teen) a device in which a large blade drops down and chops off someone's head; here, a metaphor—the nod "chops off" any more questions

habitat the type of environment in which an organism generally lives

haiku a Japanese poetic form contrasting two images, often of nature, which has 3 lines of 5, 7, and 5 syllables; spelled the same in both singular and plural forms

haughtiness snobbishness; pride

heedful carefully paying attention

hieroglyphic an ancient system of writing that includes pictures and symbols

icebox refrigerator

illumination understanding; awareness

imagery language used by a poet that encourages a reader to make mental pictures as he or she reads

images mental pictures created by a reader as he or she reads

immeasurably impossible to measure; exceedingly

industrial relating to the commercial production and sale of goods

ineffable impossible to describe

inferences reasonable guesses

inquisitorial trying to get information in a hostile, cruel, or harsh way

interact to engage with by reacting to, remembering, wondering about, asking questions of, or getting ideas from something or someone

interacting with the text "carrying on a conversation" with a text; a strategy for effective reading that involves circling, underlining, and writing notes

internment being confined, especially in wartime

intervals spaces between each point

jolt a sudden bump or jerking movement

karate a martial art, or style of self-defense, from the island of Okinawa

khaki (KAK ee) sturdy, yellowish brown cloth

la abuela [lah ah BWAY lah] the grandmother

la familia [lah fah MEE lee ah] family

la isla [lah EES lah] island

languishing losing strength; withering away

lofty high; soaring

lounge [noun] a place for people to sit and relax

lounge [verb] relax

lynch to murder by hanging

main idea [subject] + [what the author says about the subject] = main idea; the central focus of a piece of nonfiction

make inferences a reading strategy that involves making reasonable guesses by putting together something you have read in a story with something you know from real life

making connections a reading strategy that involves comparing what you are reading to something you already know

mandate to require as if, or actually, by law

mason a stoneworker; a craftsman who works with stones or bricks

mechanical relating to machines or tools; automatic

menace threat of danger

merciless showing no mercy or pity

metaphor a technique of figurative language in which one thing is described in terms of something else

meticulously carefully; with attention to detail

monolith a large block of stone

nada [NAH dah] nothing

Negro a person of African descent. NOTE: *African American* is now strongly preferred.

newsreels short films about current events

Nile The longest river in the world, flowing about 6,677 km (4,150 mi) through eastern Africa

northern lights streaks of light seen in the night sky in the northernmost parts of the northern hemisphere; aurora borealis

onslaught overwhelming amount

opposing viewpoints sides of an argument different from that of an author or speaker

Oriental Asian; from the region that includes Asia south of the Himalaya Mountains. NOTE: *Asian* is now strongly preferred.

papier-mâché (PAY per muh SHAY) a material made from paper mixed with glue or paste that can be shaped when wet and becomes hard when dry

pathos something that makes people feel sympathy or sorrow

peat partially decomposed vegetation found in bogs

peril danger

perish to die or be destroyed

periscope an instrument with lenses and mirrors that helps one see things that are not in the direct line of sight

perspective the point of view or angle from which you see a subject

persuade to try to convince others to feel the same way you do

pew a long bench of seats in a church

pharaoh a king of ancient Egypt

pillar architectural column

plight a bad or difficult situation

plot how the characters and events in a story are connected

Plymouth a car made by a company called Chrysler

poetic license bending of writing rules by a poet

point of view how one sees an event; perspective

poised balanced in readiness, waiting

political prisoner a person who has been put in jail for his or her political views prediction an educated guess about upcoming events that is based on background knowledge and clues from the present

prediction an educated guess about upcoming events that is based on background knowledge and clues from the text

protracted extended; taking place over a long time

pulverize to pound, grind, or crush into small pieces

quarry a large area from which stone is dug, blasted, or cut out

radiocarbon dating a way to determine the approximate age of an ancient object by measuring the amount of carbon-14 it contains

reeds tall grasses that grow in wet areas

reflecting taking time to think about what you have read

refuse [REF-yoos] garbage

reluctantly not eagerly

repercussions bouncing-back of sounds

repertoire a performer's collection of abilities

repertoire of skills and strategies a collection of learned abilities needed by an effective writer or reader

resolution the end of a story, in which the problems are resolved or the story gets "wrapped up"

revenge punishment of somebody in return for harm done

ridiculous silly

rising action the central part of a story during which various problems arise, leading up to the climax

rule the afternoon to have complete control over

rummaging searching hastily through the contents of a container

runners blades under a sled that help it move over snow or ice

sanitation cleanliness

Sanitation Laborer someone who cleans up garbage

scamper to run quickly and playfully

scolding yelling at; criticizing

scrupulously thoroughly; in keeping with the law or rules

sensory language language that appeals to the reader's senses

sequence the order of events

serials stories presented in installments or in a series

setting the time and place of a story

simile a technique of figurative language in which the characteristics of one thing are described in terms of something else using the word *like* or *as*

sinkhole a sunken area where waste collects

slackening easing up

solitary done alone

somber sadly serious

sorrow sadness

species a group of organisms that are similar and that can produce young that are fertile

speech a talk given to an audience

squatting crouching; sitting on one's heels

stern [adjective] strict; severe

stern [noun] the back part of a ship

steward assistant to passengers on a ship

stole a long scarf worn around the shoulders

story line the sequence of events in the order they are told in a story

strategic reader one who uses a repertoire of skills and strategies to help in understanding texts

style one's unique way of expressing oneself

subject the person, place, or thing a writer has written about in a piece of nonfiction

suffice to be sufficient or enough

support information a writer or speaker uses in trying to persuade an audience

taking notes a way to organize ideas by making short written comments about what one is reading

taunts teases; insults

taunting mocking; teasing

tic a small, repeated movement

transcendent extraordinary; going beyond the usual limits

tremor a trembling, shaking movement; a small earthquake

troubled worried; bothered

tumultuously in a way that is full of commotion; disorderly

unanimous agreed upon by all

un cero [oon SAIR oh] a zero

unconscious not aware

unfettered not restrained

unreasonable unwilling to consider another's argument

vestibule a waiting area or room

visualizing a reading strategy in which a reader makes mental pictures of what he or she is reading about

vulnerable at risk of being harmed

warming house building where people, especially skaters or skiers, come in to get warm and rest

wary cautious; worried

weave to move in and out or from side to side

weighty serious and important

wheel-dogs specially trained dogs that steer a sled (chariot) across frozen, snow-covered ground

woldwellers fictional creatures that live alone in forest trees

word choice the conscious decision of a writer to use specific words to convey an image

ACKNOWLEDGMENTS

10, 13, 20, 22 From *Before We Were Free*. Copyright © 2002 by Julia Alvarez. Published by Dell Laurel-Leaf in paperback in 2003 and originally in hardcover by Alfred A. Knopf Children's Books, a division of Random House, New York. Reprinted by permission of Susan Bergholz Literary Services, New York. All rights reserved.

18 From *Latin American Politics and Development, Fifth Edition,* by Howard J. Wiarda, Copyright © 2000 by Westview Press. Reprinted by permission of Westview Press, a member of Perseus Books, LLC.

26, 29 "All Summer in a Day" by Ray Bradbury. Reprinted by permission of Don Congdon Associates, Inc. Copyright © 1954, renewed 1982.

33, 36 "Hearing the Sweetest Songs" by Nicolette Toussaint from Newsweek 5/23/1994. All rights reserved. Reprinted by permission.

42 From *The Search for Delicious* by Natalie Babbitt. Used by permissions of Farrar, Straus and Giroux, LLC.

42 From *A Wrinkle in Time* by Madeline L'Engle. Used by permissions of Farrar, Straus and Giroux, LLC .

44, 47 From *Danny: The Champion of the World* by Roald Dahl, illustrated by Jill Bennett, text and illustrations copyright © 1975 by Roald Dahl Nominee Limited. Used by permission of Alfred A. Knopf, an imprint of Random House Children's Books, a division of Random House, Inc.

53 From *An Island Like You, Stories of the Barrio* by Judith Ortiz Cofer. Published by Orchard Books/Scholastic Inc. Copyright © 1995 by Judith Ortiz Cofer. Used by permission of Scholastic Inc.

58, 60 From *The Titanic* by Richard Wormser, text copyright © 1994. Used by permission of Parachute Publishing, L.L.C.

67, 69 From "John Thayer: Becoming a Man aboard the *Titanic*" by Phillip Hoose. Used by permission of Farrar, Straus and Giroux, LLC.

70 Jennifer Kirkpatrick/National Geographic.

72 "Karate Kid" copyright © 1996 by Jane Yolen. First appeared in *Opening Days, Short Poems,* published by Harcourt Brace. Reprinted by permission of Curtis Brown, Ltd.

75 "Skiing" copyright © 1971 by Bobbi Katz. Used with permission of the author.

77 "Swimming" from *A Tree Place And Other Poems* by Constance Levy. Copyright © 1994 Constance Levy. Used by permission of Marian Reiner for the author.

79 "The Base Stealer" by Robert Francis, from *The Orb Weaver* © 1960 and reprinted by permission of Wesleyan University Press.

81 Special permission granted by *Weekly Reader*. All rights reserved.

86 Excerpt from *A Summer to Die* by Lois Lowry. Copyright © 1977 by Lois Lowry. Reprinted by permission of Houghton Mifflin Company. All rights reserved.

89 Excerpt from *The Silent Boy* by Lois Lowry. Copyright © 2003 by Lois Lowry. Reprinted by permission of Houghton Mifflin Company. All rights reserved.

93 Excerpt from *The Giver* by Lois Lowry. Copyright © 1993 by Lois Lowry. Reprinted by permission of Houghton Mifflin Company. All rights reserved.

96 Excerpt from *Gathering Blue* by Lois Lowry. Copyright © 2000 by Lois Lowry. Reprinted by permission of Houghton Mifflin Company. All rights reserved.

99 Used by permission of Lois Lowry.

102 "Eagle Boy" from *Native American Animal Stories* told by Joseph Bruchac. Used by permission of Fulcrum Publishing.

108 "Salmon Boy" from *Native American Animal Stories* told by Joseph Bruchac. Used by permission of Fulcrum Publishing.

118 Elie Wiesel Foundation for Humanity.

119 "To You" from *The Collected Poems of Langston Hughes* by Langston Hughes, copyright © 1994 by The Estate of Langston Hughes. Used by permission of Alfred A. Knopf, a division of Random House, Inc.

121 Excerpt from *Farewell to Manzanar* by James D. Houston and Jeanne Wakatsuki Houston. Copyright © 1973 by James D. Houston. Reprinted by permission of Houghton Mifflin Company. All rights reserved.

123, 124 From *The Gold Cadillac* by Mildred D. Taylor, copyright © 1987 by Mildred D. Taylor, text. Used by permission of Dial Books for Young Readers, A Division of Penguin Young Readers Group. A Member of Penguin Group (USA) Inc., 345 Hudson Street, New York, NY 10014. All rights reserved.

132, 135 From *Egyptian Pyramids* by Anne Steel. Used by permission of Hodder & Stoughton.

138 Reprinted from *The Ancient Egyptians* by Elsa Marston with permission of Marshall Cavendish

139 From WGBH Educational Foundation, copyright © 2000 WGBH/Boston

142 From *Cat Mummies* by Kelly Trumble, illustrated by Laszlo Kubinyi. Text copyright © 1996 by Kelly Trumble. Illustrations copyright © 1996 by Laszlo Kubinyi. Reprinted by permission of Clarion Books, an imprint of Houghton Mifflin Company. All rights reserved.

144 Excerpt from *How to Make a Mummy Talk* by James M. Deem. Text copyright © 1995 by James M. Deem. Reprinted by permission of Houghton Mifflin Company. All rights reserved.

148, 151, 153 Reprinted with the permission of Atheneum Books for Young Readers, an imprint of Simon & Schuster Children's Publishing Division, from *The Egypt Game* by Zilpha Keatley Snyder. Copyright © 1967 Zilpha Keatley

156, 160 Excerpt from *Project Mulberry* by Linda Sue Park. Copyright © 2005 by Linda Sue Park. Reprinted by permission of Clarion Books, an imprint of Houghton Mifflin Company. All rights reserved.

164 From *All I Really Need to Know I Learned in Kindergarten* by Robert L. Fulghum, copyright © 1986, 1988 by Robert L. Fulghum. Used by permission of Random House, Inc.

166 George Lucas Educational Foundation

171 From *The Greatest: Muhammad Ali* by Walter Dean Myers. Published by Scholastic Inc./Scholastic Press. Copyright © 2001 by Walter Dean Myers. Reprinted by permission.

173 From *Green Planet Rescue* by Robert R. Halpern. Used by permission of The Zoological Society of Cincinnati.

175 "A Word is Dead" by Emily Dickinson. Reprinted by permission of the publishers and the Trustees of Amherst College from *The Poems of Emily Dickinson,* Thomas H. Johnson, ed., Cambridge, Mass.: The Belknap Press of Harvard University Press, Copyright © 1951, 1955, 1979,1983 by the President and Fellows of Harvard College.

176 "This Is Just to Say" by William Carlos Williams, from *Collected Poems: 1909-1939, Volume I,* copyright © 1938 by New Directions Publishing Corp. Reprinted by permission of New Directions Publishing Corp.

177 "The Red Wheelbarrow" by William Carlos Williams, from *Collected Poems: 1909-1939, Volume I,* copyright © 1938 by New Directions Publishing Corp. Reprinted by permission of New Directions Publishing Corp.

182 "Fire and Ice" from *The Poetry of Robert Frost* edited by Edward Connery Lathem. Copyright 1923, 1969 by Henry Holt and Company. Copyright 1951 by Robert Frost. Reprinted by permission of Henry Holt and Company, LLC

191 From *Guts* by Gary Paulsen, copyright © 2001 by Gary Paulsen. Used by permission of Random House Children's Books, a division of Random House, Inc.

192 From *The River* by Gary Paulsen, copyright © 1991 by Gary Paulsen. Used by permission of Dell Publishing, a division of Random House, Inc.

195, 198 From *Dancing Carl* by Gary Paulsen. Reprinted with the permission of Atheneum Books for Young Readers, an imprint of Simon & Schuster Children's Publishing Division. Copyright © 1983 Gary Paulsen.

201 From *Dogsong* by Gary Paulsen. Reprinted with the permission of Atheneum Books for Young Readers, an imprint of Simon & Schuster Children's Publishing Division. Copyright © 1985 Gary Paulsen.

204 From *Woodsong* by Gary Paulsen. Reprinted with the permission of Simon & Schuster Books for Young Readers, an imprint of Simon & Schuster Children's Publishing Division. Text copyright © 1990 Gary Paulsen

208 "Eleven" from *Woman Hollering Creek and Other Stories* by Sandra Cisneros. Used by permission of Random House.

214 "My Name" from *The House on Mango Street* by Sandra Cisneros. Used by permission of Random House.

ILLUSTRATIONS

137: © Great Source; **142** *m:* © Laszlo Kubinyi. Reprinted by permission of Houghton Mifflin Company. All rights reserved.
All additional art created by AARTPACK, Inc.

PHOTOGRAPHY

Photo Research AARTPACK, Inc.

Unit 1 9: © Kris Timken/Getty Image; **10:** © Ryan McVay/Getty Images; **11:** © Ryan McVay/Getty Images; **12:** © Martin Hospach/Getty Images; **13:** © Royalty-Free/Corbis; **14:** © Royalty-Free/Corbis; **15:** © Royalty-Free/Corbis; **16:** © Royalty-Free/Corbis; **17:** © Ryan McVay/Getty Images; **18:** © Ryan McVay/Getty Images; **20 t:** © PhotoDisc/Getty Images; **20 b:** © PhotoDisc/Getty Images; **22:** © Royalty-Free/Corbis; **23:** © PhotoDisc/Getty Images; **24:** Royalty-Free/Corbis.

Unit 2 25: © Lawrence Lawry/Getty Images; **26:** © Royalty-Free/Corbis; **27:** © PhotoDisc/Getty Images; **28:** © Royalty-Free/Corbis; **29:** © Shaen Adey/Gallo Images/Getty Images; **31:** © Shaen Adey/Gallo Images/Getty Images; **32:** © Royalty-Free/Corbis; **33:** © DynamicGraphics Inc./Inmagine; 34: © MedioImages/Getty Images; **35:** © Dynamic-Graphics Inc./Inmagine; **36:** © Pixtal/Inmagine; **37:** © Royalty-Free/Corbis; **38 t:** © MedioImages/Getty Images; **38:** © Pixtal/Inmagine; **39:** © Royalty-Free/Corbis; **40:** © Royalty-Free/Corbis.

Unit 3 41: © Teri Dixon/Getty Images; **42:** © Adalberto Rios Szalay/Sexto Sol/Getty Images; **44:** © Wilfried Krecichwost/Getty Images; **45:** © Wilfried Krecichwost/Getty Images; **47:** © Royalty-Free/Corbis; **48:** © Royalty-Free/Corbis; **49 b:** © DesignPics/Inmagine; **50:** © Brand X Pictures/Inmagine; **51:** © Image Source/Getty Images; **53:** © Image Source/Getty Images; **55:** © Image Source/Getty Images.

Unit 4 57: © Diane Macdonald/getty Images; **58 m:** © Sun Source/The Baltimore Sun; **58 l:** © Royalty-Free/Corbis; **60:** ©PhotoDisc/Getty Images; **61:** ©PhotoDisc/Getty Images; **64:** © Royalty-Free/Corbis; **65:** © Royalty-Free/Corbis; **66:** © Royalty-Free/Corbis; **67:** © Royalty-Free/Corbis; **69:** © Royalty-Free/Corbis; **70 t:** © Royalty-Free/Corbis; **70 b:** © Stockdisc/Getty Images.

Unit 5 71: © Angelo Cavalli/Getty Images; **72 t:** © IndexStock/Inmagine; **72 m:** © TongRo/Inmagine; **72 b:** © Natphotos/Getty Images; **73:** © IndexStock/Inmagine; **74:** © Natphotos/Getty Images; **75:** © Royalty-Free/Corbis;

76: © Royalty-Free/Corbis; **77:** © DAJ/Getty Images; **78:** © DAJ/getty Images; **79:** © Royalty-Free/Corbis; **80:** © Royalty-Free/Corbis; **81:** © Nancy R Cohen/Getty Images; **82:** © Royalty-Free/Corbis; **83:** © PhotoDisc/Getty Images; **84:** © PhotoDisc/Getty Images.

Unit 6 85: © Colin Hawkins/Getty Images; **86:** © Erin Hogan/Getty Images; **87:** © PhotoDisc/Getty Images; **88:** © PhotoDisc/Getty Images; **89:** © Royalty-Free/Corbis; **90:** © Royalty-Free/Corbis; **91:** © Digital Zoo/Getty Images; **92 t:** © PhotoDisc/Getty Images; **92 m:** © Image Source/Getty Images; **93:** © Tim Hibo/Getty Images; **96:** © Royalty-Free/Corbis; **97:** © Royalty-Free/Corbis; **99:** © Royalty-Free/Corbis; **100:** © Royalty-Free/Corbis.

Unit 7 101: © Hisham F Ibrahim/Getty Images; **102:** © Medioimages/Getty Images; **103:** © Tom Brakefield/Getty Images; **104:** © Tom Brakefield/Getty Images; **106:** © Tom Brakefield/Getty Images; **107:** © Tom Brakefield/Getty Images; **108:** © Diana Miller/Getty Images; **109:** © Diana Miller/Getty Images; **110:** © Diana Miller/Getty Images; **111:** © Royalty-Free/Corbis; **112:** © Charles C Place/Getty Images; **113:** © Bettmann/Corbis; **114:** © Univ of Washington Libraries, Special Collections, NA 2463; **115:** © PhotoDisc/Inmagine; **116:** © Univ of Washington Libraries, Special Collections, NA 2210.

Unit 8 117: © Royalty-Free/Corbis; **118 l:** © John Wang/Getty Images; **118 b:** © John Wang/Getty Images; **119:** © John Wang/Getty Images; **120:** © PhotoDisc/Getty Images; **121:** © Itaru Hirama/Getty Images; **123:** © Comstock/Inmagine; **124:** © Royalty-Free/Corbis; **125:** © Royalty-Free/Corbis; **126:** © Royalty-Free/Corbis; **127:** © Royalty-Free/Corbis; **128:** © Mike Spring/Getty Images; **129:** © Comstock/Inmagine; **130:** © Brand X Pictures.

Unit 9 131: © GDT/Getty Images; **132 t:** © Petr Svarc/Getty Images; **132 b:** © Petr Svarc/Getty Images; **133 t:** © Adam Crowley/Getty Images; **133 ml:** © Royalty-Free/Corbis; **133 mlc:** © Royalty-Free/Corbis; **133 mrc:** © Royalty-Free/Corbis; **133 mr:** © Royalty-Free/Corbis; **134:** © Petr Svarc/Getty Images; **135 t:** © Derek P Redfearn/Getty Images; **135 b:** © Derek P Redfearn/Getty Images; **136:** © Brand X Pictures/Inmagine; **137:** © Adam

Crowley/Getty Images; **138:** © Gerard Rollando/ Getty Images; **139:** © Pankaj & Insy Shah/Getty Images; **141:** © Gerard Rollando/Getty Images; **142 *t*:** © Alistair Duncan/Getty Images; **143 *t*:** © Derek P Redfearn/Getty Images; **143 *b*:** © Pankaj & Insy Shah/Getty Images; **144 *m*:** © www.mummytombs.com; **144 *l*:** © PhotoDisc/Getty Images; **146:** © Adam Crowley/Getty Images.

Unit 10 **147:** © Royalty-Free/Corbis; **148:** © Royalty-Free/Corbis; **149:** © Royalty-Free/ Corbis; **150:** © Stockbyte/Getty Images; **151:** © Izzy Schwartz/Getty Images; **152:** © PhotoDisc/Getty Images; **153:** © Gordon Osmundson/Corbis; **154:** © Royalty-Free/Corbis; **155:** © Gordon Osmundson/Corbis; **156:** © Brand X Pictures/ Inmagine; **157:** © DAJ/Getty Images; **158:** © Izzy Schwartz/Getty Images; **159:** © Jeff Greenberg/ Photo Edit; **160:** © David Young-Wolff/Photo Edit; **161:** © DAJ/Getty Images; **162 *t*:** © Jeff Greenberg/ Photo Edit; **162 *b*:** © Jeff Greenberg/Photo Edit.

Unit 11 **163:** © Alain Pons/Getty Images; **164:** © Sheila Terry/Photo Researchers, Inc.; **165:** © Royalty-Free/Corbis; **166:** © PhotoDisc/ Inmagine; **167:** © PhotoDisc/Inmagine; **168:** © Royalty-Free/Corbis; **169:** © Comstock/ Jupiter Images; **171 *t*:** © Bettmann/Corbis; **171 *b*:** © PhotoDisc/Getty Images; **172:** © Rim Light/PhotoLink/Getty Images; **173 *t*:** © Spike Mafford/Getty Images; **173 *b*:** © Royalty-Free/ Corbis; **174:** © PhotoDisc/Getty Images.

Unit 12 **175:** © Royalty-Free/Corbis; **176:** © Royalty-Free/Corbis; **177:** © Royalty-Free/ Corbis; **178:** © PhotoDisc/Getty Images; **179:** © Comstock Images; **180:** © Don Farrall/Getty Images; **181:** © PhotoDisc/Getty Images;

182 *t*: © Royalty-Free/Corbis; **182 *b*:** © Karl Weatherly/Getty Images; **183:** © Karl Weatherly/Getty Images; **184 *t*:** © Tom Brakefield/Getty Images; **184 *m*:** © Tom Brakefield/Getty Images; **185:** © Royalty-Free/Corbis; **186:** © Royalty-Free/ Corbis; **187:** © Royalty-Free/Corbis; **188:** © Royalty-Free/Corbis; **189:** © Don Farrall/Getty Images; **190:** © PhotoDisc/Getty Images.

Unit 13 **191:** © Robert Cable/Getty Images; **192:** © PhotoDisc/Getty Images; **193:** © Maurice Joseph/ Getty Images; **194:** © PhotoDisc/Getty Images; **195:** © Steve Mason/Getty Images; **196:** © Royalty-Free/Corbis; **197:** © Steve Mason/Getty Images; **198:** © Royalty-Free/Corbis; **199:** © Royalty-Free/ Corbis; **200:** © DesignPics/Inmagine; **201:** © Royalty-Free/Corbis; **202:** © Royalty-Free/ Corbis; **203:** © John A Rizzo/Getty Images; **204:** © Royalty-Free/Corbis; **206:** © Royalty-Free/ Corbis.

Unit 14 **207:** © Royalty-Free/Corbis; **208:** © Royalty-Free/Corbis; **209:** © Royalty-Free/ Corbis; **210 *t*:** © Kent Knudson/PhotoLink/Getty Images; **210 *m*:** © Brand X Pictures; **210 *b*:** © Kent Knudson/PhotoLink/Getty Images; **211:** © Royalty-Free/Corbis; **212:** © Royalty-Free/Corbis; **214 *t*:** © Royalty-Free/Corbis; **214 *b*:** © Royalty-Free/Corbis; **215 *t*:** © Laurent Hamels/Getty Images; **215 *m*:** © Laurent Hamels/Getty Images; **215 *b*:** © Laurent Hamels/Getty Images; **216:** © Royalty-Free/Corbis; **217:** © Ken Usami/ Getty Images; **218 *l*:** © Ken Usami/Getty Images; **218 *r*:** © Nigel Hillier/Getty Images; **218 *m*:** © PhotoDisc/Getty Images.

Becoming an Active Reader **221:** © Image Source/Getty Images; **222–224:** © Kaz Chiba/ PhotoDisc/Getty Images; **225:** © Jamie Kripke/ Getty Images.

INDEX